CLASSIC REPRINT

HISTORY
of the
Blackburn Rovers
Football Club
1875 to 1925

By

CHARLES FRANCIS

INTRODUCTION

When, in 1925, Mr. Charles Francis wrote this 50-year history of Blackburn Rovers FC, it was among the earliest detailed club histories to be published. Original copies of this little gem of a book are now very rare indeed so we have decided to add this title to our expanding *Classic Reprint* series. This, we hope, will give more readers the opportunity to learn about the origins and early history of this distinguished club.

We have endeavoured to keep the page format and styling of this reprint as close as possible to the original book and have also included all the illustrations. Regrettably, the illustrations were not of the highest quality in the original book and our reproductions reflect this.

British Library Cataloguing in Publication Data
A catalogue record for this book is available from the British Library

ISBN 1-86223-117-6

Copyright © 2005, SOCCER BOOKS LIMITED. (01472 696226)
72 St. Peter's Avenue, Cleethorpes, N.E. Lincolnshire, DN35 8HU, England

www.soccer-books.co.uk

Printed by 4Edge Limited

CONTENTS

THE BOARD OF DIRECTORS.

STANDING: J. CARR (SECRETARY-MANAGER), W. TEMPEST, R. CROMPTON, J. H. CHADBURN, J. EDDLESTON, J.P. (VICE-CHAIRMAN), T. BIRTWISTLE.
SITTING: W. H. GRIMSHAW, J. H. FORREST, J. W. WALSH (CHAIRMAN), J. FORBES, J. COTTON.

PREFACE

It is a happy circumstance that coincident with its golden jubilee, which occurs this month, the Blackburn Rovers' F.C. still occupies an honoured position in the great game it has done so much to develop and popularise. Its name and deeds are indissolubly linked with the rise and progress of Association football in Great Britain and beyond the seas. From its ranks have sprung many celebrated players, officials and legislators, who have rendered eminent service in their respective spheres.

Noted for their sportsmanship and their generous support of deserving causes, the Rovers can justly be described as one of the most highly esteemed clubs in the country. By playing the game fairly and squarely they have achieved a magnificent reputation, jealously guarded by those responsible for the management of the club's affairs. With a continuance of the enterprising policy which distinguishes the Board of Directors, combined with loyalty and enthusiasm on the part of the players and backed by the whole-hearted support of the public, no misgivings need be entertained regarding the future. Animated by the glorious example of the past and imbued with the spirit to conquer, there is every reason to suppose that the club will enhance its prestige in the new era it is now privileged to enter.

In this volume, published by the Rovers' F.C. in commemoration of the golden jubilee, the history of the past 50 years is presented in narrative form, with interesting stories and piquant details woven into the text. It was contributed by the writer to *The Blackburn Times*. The articles, which have been amplified in some cases, are reproduced by the courteous permission of the

Proprietors of *The Times*. To many friends, including a colleague, W. K. Baxter, who wrote two of the post-war chapters, I tender sincere thanks for information and assistance willingly supplied and rendered, also to Messrs. Burton and Garland, Ltd., for kind permission to use their copyright photographs. C. F.

November, 1925.

HISTORY OF THE ROVERS FOOTBALL CLUB.

CHAPTER 1. — EARLY DAYS.

Historic Meeting at the St. Leger — Famous Blackburn Amateurs — Links with Malvern School — Feud with Darwen — L.F.A. Boycotted — Quaint Extracts from Early Minutes.

DURING the past 50 years the Blackburn Rovers' F.C. has been noted for its high traditions, implanted by its founders, all amateurs, who played the game for the keen enjoyment they derived from the exhilarating pastime. Their successors have worthily upheld and enhanced the prestige gained by the early "Blue and Whites," whose prowess is still the subject of conversation in sporting circles all over the world. In the back blocks of the Antipodes, on the Canadian prairies, and in faraway China and Japan their stirring deeds on the football field are discussed as eagerly as in factories, shops and offices in the homeland. On the Continent of Europe and on the South African veldt the Rovers are almost as well known as on their native heath.

Despite what critics may aver, football is a wonderful institution, and is a power for good, not only in this country but in other lands. In helping to foster this great national and international pastime Blackburn Rovers have rendered important service, though it must be confessed that when the club was started its promoters, even the most far-sighted and optimistic, had little idea of the magnitude the game was destined to attain. Its growth has been phenomenal and its popularity has surpassed the most sanguine expectations.

When the Rovers appeared on the scene, however, no frenzied shouts heralded their advent. They were an unknown quantity, and had to win their spurs. The distinction of founding the club belongs to Mr. John Lewis, who came to Blackburn from Market Drayton, his birthplace, in 1868. No purely Association football was played at that time in East Lancashire, though there was a recreation, a mixture of Rugby and Association, known as the Harrow game, at which the youth of the town, including Mr. A. N. Hornby, were experts. Mr. Lewis, though, was keen on Association without any admixture and was anxious to see it established locally. Accordingly he discussed the matter with Mr. Arthur Constantine, an old boy of Shrewsbury School. They resolved to form a Blackburn club, for which purpose they issued invitations to a meeting destined to be memorable in the sporting history of Blackburn. On that occasion a gathering of seventeen assembled at the St. Leger Hotel, on November 5th, 1875. All present, including several young fellows who had just finished their education at public schools, signified their willingness to participate in the game and the motion to create a club was carried unanimously.

Of those who attended the inaugural meeting all have passed away except Mr. Richard Birtwistle, now of Lytham; Mr. Walter Duckworth, of Blackpool and Preston; and Mr. Lewis, who resides in Gorse-road. Mr. Duckworth, who was educated at Clitheroe Grammar School, was the first secretary; Mr. Lewis was appointed treasurer, and Mr. Thos. Greenwood was the first of a long line of captains. Remembering the spacious ground at Ewood Park, now the headquarters of the club, it is instructive to recall that for the first season the Blackburn Rovers did not possess a playing pitch. Those at the helm recognised the wisdom of economy, or, at all events, were disinclined to launch out until they discovered by experience whether the new venture was likely to prove a success. Evidently they wished to make sure that the enthusiasm displayed at the outset was not a flash in the pan. There was difficulty, too,

Photo by F. Sharples, Blackburn

JOHN LEWIS.

in getting a suitable piece of land. After the officials had been selected, a team was collected and a fixture list arranged, with such clubs as Church, Darwen, Cob Wall, and Turton. That there was a demand for Association half a century ago is shown by the fact that there were plenty of candidates for vacancies occurring in the team. Indeed, members or modern directorates will be interested to learn that even in those far-off days the lot of an official was not exactly a bed of roses, for when a player was dropped or rested he was in the habit of retaliating by bluntly telling the committee that their judgment was hopelessly at fault, while officials who happened to be players as well, had many warm quarters of an hour with irate colleagues burning under a sense of injustice because their demands for inclusion had been ignored.

These spasmodic bickerings, annoying though they were at the time, did not prejudicially affect the side, who quickly demonstrated that they were not to be lightly regarded. Though always playing on foreign soil, unknown grounds did not upset the nerves or minimise the skill of the wearers of the blue and white jerseys. On the contrary, they proved such formidable opponents that they completed the first season without losing a match. The custom then was to play six forwards and two half-backs, behind whom were a pair of backs and a goalkeeper. It was not an ideal formation, because against a powerful attack too much work was thrown on the rearguard. Nottingham Forest had a different arrangement, fielding five forwards, two half-backs, two three-quarter backs, one full-back and a goalkeeper. In course of time these styles were discarded in favour of the present field formation, pioneered by Blackburn Olympic.

The men who figured in the side during the first two seasons included T. Greenwood, captain (goal); J. Baldwin and F. Birtwistle (backs); A. Thomas and T. J. Sycelmore (half-backs); W. H. Duckworth, John Lewis, Tom Dean, Harry Greenwood, Arthur Constantine, and Richard Birtwistle (forwards). In those days there were two centre-forwards, and these positions were filled by Messrs. Birtwistle and Lewis, both noted for their dash and shooting ability. Later Mr. Lewis moved to inside-left. Subsequently a skating accident terminated his career as a player. He then took up the whistle, and earned the title of "Prince of Referees." For fifty years he has been intimately connected with the great winter pastime as player, referee, legislator, and commissioner, while his knowledge of the laws of the game is probably unrivalled. Mr. Lewis is a vice-president of the Football Association, senior vice-president of the Football League, one of the three founders of the Lancashire F.A., of which he is now the president, and he is also president of the Lancashire Combination. These are a few of the offices he occupies. Few men, if any, have rendered more distinguished service to Association football than Mr. Lewis. In 1920 he was in charge of the F.A. team that toured South Africa, and never had their colours lowered, and in a similar capacity he accompanied the F.A. side that last April left our shores for Australia, where the Tourists won all their 25 matches (including five Test games), scoring 139 goals against 13.

Mr. Birtwistle formerly assisted Cob Wall. A wholehearted enthusiast, he was a skilful member of the attack. His speed was a decided asset when he was heading for goal, and he was a deadly marksman. At Blackburn, on March 30th, 1880, he had the distinction of scoring all the five goals by which the Rovers vanquished Nottingham Forest. On the running track Mr. Birtwistle won many races. An old and valued member of the Lancashire Football Association, he attended the first meeting of that body in 1878, and served on the committee for a year. Then there was a break, but since 1901 his official connection with the county association has been uninterrupted. Mr. Birtwistle has taken an active part in the management of Blackburn Rovers' F.C., first as a member of the committee, and afterwards as chairman, which position he relinquished in 1905. His son, Mr. H. H. Birtwistle, has also served the club as a director. Since the early 80's Mr. Birtwistle has attended every F.A. Cup final, and is a well-known figure at Ewood Park, where he delights in the success of his favourite team.

RICHARD BIRTWISTLE.

The Greenwood family played an important part in the rise of Association football in the Blackburn district. There were five brothers, viz., Mr. Wm. Greenwood, who used to live in Wellington-street (St. John's), whose figure on horseback was a familiar sight in the town for many years; Mr. Richard Greenwood, who resided at The Gables, Preston New-road, and at one time was president of the Cotton Employers' Association; Mr. Thomas Greenwood, Mr. Harry Greenwood, and Mr. D. H. Greenwood. It is with the last three that we are particularly concerned, for they were playing members of the Rovers. "D.H.," the youngest and most famous of the trio, was "capped" against Scotland and Ireland in 1882. As a full-back he gave many grand displays for the "Blue and Whites." Thomas had the distinction of being captain of the side from its inception down to the end of the season 1878-79. Harry was a useful half-back. Jack Baldwin belonged to a well-known Blackburn family, and his partner at back, Fred Birtwistle, hailed from Great Harwood. Arthur Thomas was the brother of Alderman F. T. Thomas, and their sister married Mr. Thomas Greenwood. The other half-back, T. J. Sycelmore, who was a Bachelor of Arts, was a master at the Grammar School. Tom Dean, who figured in the attack, was an uncle of Lieut.-Commander Percy T. Dean, V.C. Sir John Rutherford was also a playing member for a period. He was a capital half-back. At the club bazaar, in 1895, he declared that "as better players came to the front I had to drop out." That, however, was merely his modest way of accounting for his retirement. With his colleagues Sir John was very popular, and the team were exceedingly sorry to lose his services.

The brothers Jack and Fred Hargreaves, who joined the side on leaving school, were a versatile pair. Both gained international honours. Their father was the Blackburn Coroner. Fred won his laurels as a half-back, and Jack was bracketed with the best forwards of his day, being equally at home on either wing. One of his partners was A. L. Birch, son of the Vicar of Blackburn, who was specially noted for his skill as a dribbler. With D. H.

Greenwood, the brothers Hargreaves formed a trinity of Old Malvernians playing for the Rovers at the same time.

Mr. Greenwood's earliest recollection of football was when he played for his junior House eleven at Malvern and had orders from the captain to "go for the man and never mind the ball." He did so to the extent that his little finger was damaged and his nose was knocked out of shape. The only time he remembers to have been absolutely "done" was in 1879 when the Rovers played four matches (Stoke, Notts, The Pilgrims and Clapham Rovers) in five days, with a hard day's walking in London in between. They managed to avert defeat, and a huge crowd gave them a warm welcome at the station on their return home. His last match was either at Burnley or Padiham in a semi-final for the Lancashire Cup, in which he received a crack on the shin that laid him up for nearly six months. At the time he was a pupil on a farm at Tattenhall, Cheshire. On recovering from his injury he was walking over the farm with the farmer when the latter, in response to his companion's challenge, laid 10 to 1 in shillings that Mr. Greenwood could not jump a five-barred gate. The old Rover got over but just touched. An argument then arose as to "jumping" and "clearing," as a result of which he did not receive his reward! There is another interesting link between Malvern School and the Blackburn club, because the pretty colours of the Rovers were adapted from those worn at Malvern, the green of the white quartered school shirts being changed to blue, which is now of a lighter shade than that first chosen, though it is no longer fashionable to wear the dandy "nightcaps" which completed the costume of the original members of the team.

Though they played a few matches on the old cricket field at Pleasington, the Rovers had not a ground of their own until they rented a piece of farm land facing Preston New-road, part of which is now occupied by the West End Garage. On entering into possession the committee were somewhat dismayed to find that the playing pitch contained a large depression, known as a cow-pit, in which water collected for the farm stock. Naturally matches could not take place until that obstacle was removed. Nowadays such a hollow would be filled in, but those in authority solved the difficulty by roofing it with planks obtained from Mr. Duckworth's father, who was a timber merchant. The planks were then camouflaged with sods. One wonders what would have happened if the timber had given way. Luckily no such accident occurred. Otherwise the club's career might have terminated suddenly and ingloriously. This ground was vacated in favour of the Alexandra Meadows. Another move was to Leamington-road (opened on October 8th, 1881), and finally to Ewood Park. which has been the headquarters of the club since the autumn of 1890.

The famous Scottish team, Partick, visited Blackburn for the opening game on the Meadows, on January 2nd, 1878, and the event was rendered additionally noteworthy by A. N. Hornby making his initial appearance with the Rovers. To the joy of their supporters the "Blue and Whites" were victorious by 2–1, "Dick" Birtwistle scoring both goals for Blackburn. "Monkey" Hornby, a nickname by which he was affectionately known long after he left Harrow, had a great reception. Superbly built and absolutely fearless, his athletic prowess made him the idol of the Blackburn sporting public. He is best remembered, however, not as an exponent of the Association code, but as an international Rugby player, and as a champion cricketer. "A.N." was also a handy man with the gloves and at local fairs was in the habit of pitting his science against professional bruisers, many of whom he "put to sleep," to the unbounded delight of his admirers, who assembled in large numbers to see fair play, and cheer on their redoubtable hero. A universal favourite, this prince of cricket captains endeared himself to all by his genial and sunny disposition.

Curiously enough, Mr. Hornby was one of the innocent causes of the feud that developed between the Rovers and Darwen, a dramatic episode of which was the fracas between Marshall (Darwen) and Suter (Blackburn), on the Alexandra Meadows, in November, 1880. The Rovers, due to meet the Peaceful Valley eleven in a cup-tie, were anxious to strengthen their side by the inclusion of Mr. Hornby at half-back. As there was some doubt as to his eligibility, the point was referred to the County Association, who returned the following answer: "Play him if you wish, and we will consider the matter afterwards." The sting in this reply lay in the circumstance that the Rovers had grounds for believing that the Association had given a definite opinion when consulted by Darwen in a similar case respecting W. Kirkham. The position was further complicated by the county authorities ordering the tie to take place at Darwen, which was regarded as another injustice to Blackburn. So incensed were the Rovers' committee that they contemplated declining to fulfil the fixture, but, on cooling down, wiser counsels prevailed, and the match was played as arranged, though Mr. Hornby was omitted, owing to the peculiar conduct of the Lancashire Association.

So keen was the rivalry between these neighbouring clubs that there was always the danger of a spark creating a conflagration when they met. Before the sensational encounter on the Meadows in November, 1880, when the friction had become acute, Fred Hargreaves, captain of the Rovers, took the precaution of addressing his men before they went on the field, advising them to give no cause for offence. The ground was packed with spectators, estimated at 10,000, an unusually large number for those days; the stand was filled, twenty lorries provided extra platform accommodation, and seats were placed inside the boundary ropes. In the first half the crowd twice broke through the ropes; otherwise there were no unseemly incidents, and the teams crossed over with the score 1–1. Kirkham had opened the visitors' account after twenty-three minutes, and Duckworth had equalised from a centre by Brown, who before parting with the ball dribbled nearly the whole length of the field. In the second period play had been in progress eight minutes when Marshall, on being robbed of the ball by Suter (who had captained the Darwen side the previous season) seized the Blackburn back in his arms and threw him down near the spectators. The crowd, promptly invading the field, separated the combatants, but there was such an uproar that

A. N. HORNBY.

the match had to be abandoned. The referee, Mr. Sam Ormerod, according to a published statement, was credited with having said in reference to the two players chiefly concerned, that "it was six of one and half-a-dozen of the other," though he did not accuse Suter of an unfair charge, which the visitors alleged was the cause of the fracas, and which was strenuously denied by Suter. All sorts of rumours were afloat afterwards, including the assertion that the game was purposely broken up to prevent either side winning. A gentleman present at the match told the writer that his impression was that the spectators temporarily lost their heads, in consequence of the dispute between the two players, and that the position was aggravated by the extreme rivalry between the clubs. Whatever the correct version may be, the fact remains that the hatchet was not buried until the beginning of 1882.

In the meantime there were several disputes between Darwen and the Rovers. One of them related to a Lancashire Cup-tie, and the County Association marked their displeasure by excluding both clubs from the competition. The Rovers, contending that they were in no way to blame, retaliated by boycotting the Association. They induced celebrated Scottish teams to visit them on dates fixed for the Lancashire Cup ties, and by this means decoyed nearly all the football enthusiasts in the district. Their jubilation can be imagined when the final for the Lancashire Cup attracted but a handful of spectators, the game being played at Darwen, with Park Road and Accrington as the contestants. Vale of Leven were the counter-attraction at Blackburn. The Lancashire F.A. suffered so severely in their exchequer that at last they approached the Football Association to obtain their aid in extricating them from their unfortunate position. As a consequence peace was restored.

But further trouble loomed ahead. On a complaint by Darwen that the Rovers would not fulfil a fixture, representatives of the Blackburn club were directed to appear before the F.A. in London. Dr. Morley, vice-president of the club and brother of Viscount Morley of Blackburn, and Mr. John Lewis, then the hon. secretary, were sent as delegates. All who knew the late Dr. Morley are aware

Dr. E. S. MORLEY.

of his pugnacious disposition. He was famous not only for his cigars and his velvet coats, but for the strength of his convictions, which he was in the habit of freely expressing. If the F.A. expected they were receiving a couple of penitents when the vice-president and secretary of the Rovers were ushered into the room they were soon undeceived. It was Dr. Morley's introduction to the Football Association (of which he later became a vice-president), and when he confronted the Council he staggered the members by curtly addressing them as follows :— "We have come in deference to your wishes, but I want to point out to you that you have no authority to call upon us to come in connection with a dispute between Darwen and ourselves, nor have you any right to enter into that dispute. At the same time, we are not afraid of the strictest and fullest investigation into our conduct in this matter, as we assert that we are not to blame for the trouble that has occurred." Major Marindin was in the chair, and after the Council had recovered from their astonishment at the doctor's uncompromising declaration, they called on Darwen to state their case. When the decision was announced in favour of Blackburn, the Rovers' delegates felt that they had worthily discharged the duty entrusted to them.

Dr. Morley's connection with the Rovers dated from 1880. He was quickly made a vice-president, a position he occupied until the club was floated, when he was elected chairman of the directors, a post he retained until failing health precluded his attendance at the meetings, but up to his death he had a seat on the directorate. Old-timers will remember his famous slogan: "For heaven's sake, Rovers, play FOOTBALL!"

The early balance sheets of the club offer a sharp contrast to the vast sums spent on modern football. For the first season the income was £2 8s., made up entirely of members' subscriptions. As the club were without a ground there were no gate receipts. The treasurer was in the enviable position of being able to balance his accounts, because the expenditure was not allowed to exceed the income. The outlay included 8s. 10d. for goalposts and 15s. for a football, which was the only one the team possessed. There were, of course, no wages for players. In 1876-7 the receipts had risen to £8 12s. 6d., including the handsome sum of 6/6 for "gate" money. Expenditure had increased to £9 6s. 4d. The minute book records that "tape for goal" cost 2/-, "leather football case" 6/-, and "football from Preston" 11/-. Four flags ran away with 3/8, while a policeman whose services were requisitioned to regulate the crowd on December 16th, 1876 (when the first and only "gate" of the season realised 6/6), was rewarded with the munificent allowance of 4d.! The next season the treasurer was in a position to present a more satisfactory financial statement, owing to increased "gates," such as £2 14s. when Turton were at Blackburn, £7 18s. from a match with Darwen, 16/6 from a game with Clitheroe, and £1 0s. 9d. when Cob Wall were entertained. An important event was the visit of Partick. The receipts on that occasion amounted to £25 6s., which, however, did not quite cover the expenses. The payments to police for services rendered jumped from 4d. to 6/3, and the club finished with a balance of £1 16s. 6d.

For the first season the subscription for members was 3/-; this was increased to 5/- in the second season, while at the general meeting on August 30th, 1878, Mr. Arthur Thomas presiding, it was resolved "That on the election of any member he shall be supplied with a copy of the Association Rules, together with our rules, with this addition: 'That any member not having paid his subscription within one month after election shall cease to be a member.'" In 1878-9 the club had 85 members. By then matches had been played with Darwen, Church, Turton, Preston Rovers, Cob Wall, Eagley, St. George's (Blackburn), Clitheroe, Partick, Sheffield, Manchester Wanderers, Macclesfield Rangers, Blackburn Olympic and Padiham. A second eleven was formed in 1876, and in December should have gone to Church, but the minute book says "only five men were at the railway station," so, apparently, the fixture was not fulfilled.

CHAPTER II. — AMAZING SCORING FEATS.

A Galaxy of Stars — "Johnny" Forbes Becomes a Rover — Science v. Brute Force — The Scottish Invasion — "Jimmy" Forrest as Boy International — "Herby" Arthur's Brilliant Career — How Rovers Lost J. W. Crabtree.

DURING the glorious period in the 'eighties when the Rovers began to make history, they performed some astonishing feats of goal-scoring. It was usual for them to defeat opponents by a double-figure total. "Proud Preston" would long retain vivid memories of their first encounter with the "Blue and Whites," for they were beaten 16–0 in March, 1881, by the following team: A. Woolfall, goal; H. McIntyre and D. Greenwood, backs; F. Hargreaves and H. Sharples, half-backs; J. Duckworth and J. Douglas, right wing; J. Brown and T. Jefferson, centres; G. Avery and J. Hargreaves, left wing. The match was played at Preston, the visitors scoring eight goals in each half, but the newspaper report only particularises the first five, which were obtained by Brown (2), J. Hargreaves (2), and Avery.

One can picture the forlornness of Sheffield Park Grange on leaving the field at Blackburn, routed to the tune of 17–0 (October, 1884), while just to convince sceptics that that amazing victory was not accidental, the Rovers two days afterwards subdued Rossendale by 11 clear goals. Some years later Rhyl received the shock of their lives when their Lancashire visitors piled up 16 goals, though the Welshmen managed to save their face by scoring three times. Blackburn Park-road and Kirkham were each vanquished 14–0 in one season. Others who shared a somewhat similar fate were Great

Harwood (13–3), Blackburn Olympic (12–1), Notts County (10–1), and Liverpool (also 10–1). In two successive seasons Blackpool were defeated 11–1. Leeds were completely nonplussed when the Rovers penetrated their defence a dozen times, without allowing the Yorkshiremen to reply. Withnell also suffered a 12–0 reverse, but North End did a little better, scoring two goals against the 12 registered by their opponents. The "Blue and Whites" celebrated Queen Victoria's golden jubilee by scoring 11 goals against Manchester, and 10 against Bury, without their own defence being pierced. The players responsible for these notable achievements included such artistes as Jack Hargreaves, Jimmy Brown, Geo. Avery, Tod. Strachan, Jimmy Douglas, Joe Lofthouse, Herbert Fecitt, Joe Sowerbutts, Jock lnglis, Nat. Walton, J. Heyes, Billy Townley, Jack Southworth, and W. Almond.

In this galaxy of stars Brown and Southworth earned undying fame as centre-forwards. Brown's dribbling was so wonderful that his admirers were in the habit of saying that "the ball must be tied to his bootlaces." He was a brilliant individualist. Southworth, though, led the forward line with even greater judgment and skill, and was a more successful marksman. He has been described by competent judges as the best of all English centre-forwards. When a mere boy of 16 he was such a deadly shot that he scored six goals for Blackburn Olympic against Leigh. After he donned the Rovers' colours custodians had every reason to fear his ability. For instance, against Sheffield Wednesday, who were beaten 5–2 in May, 1890, he registered all the Blackburn goals, but his outstanding achievement was performed after he had joined Everton, when, within ten days, he was responsible for 15 of 22 goals scored in four matches, including six in succession against West Bromwich Albion.

Among the sporting attractions in the "good old days" were the visits of celebrated Scottish teams, who generally came south at the New Year. The games aroused unusual interest among football enthusiasts in this district. Queen's Park was one of the clubs that went on tour. A good story is connected with their first appearance at Blackburn. They were offered the choice of a guarantee or half the "gate." It was explained to them that if the weather was favourable there would certainly be a large attendance, but the canny Scots preferred a lump sum. Therefore it was agreed that "Queen's" should receive £25 for the trip. Fortunately for the Rovers the climatic conditions were all that could be desired, the receipts exceeding £400. Thus in place of drawing a cool £200 the visitors pocketed an eighth of that amount. On the homeward journey they would probably reflect that in this instance they had carried financial caution to excess.

Resenting the growing popularity of these fixtures, the "Scottish Athletic Journal" uncharitably suggested that "none of the really first-class organisations have crossed the Border during the present holidays (1888), doubtless recognising that little is to be gained and much in the shape of prestige lost by embarking on excursions of this kind at a time when all the world is given to festivity and frivolity." In an effective rejoinder "The Blackburn Times" declared that for the "Journal" to exclude Cambuslang, Heart of Midlothian, Partick and other noted clubs from the first flight was about as foolish as the classification of the Rovers at the beginning of the season as a "second rate" organisation, adding that when Lancashire sides went north they generally managed to "thrash the teams "who had the honour of belonging to the exclusive set.

It was as a direct consequence of these holiday jaunts that "Johnny" Forbes became a Blackburn Rover. This famous left-back, probably without a rival as an exponent of pure football, when on tour with Vale of Leven accepted an invitation to assist the "Blue and Whites" against the formidable Corinthians, who had enlisted the services of another brilliant back in "Watty" Arnott, of Queen's Park. Only one goal was scored on that April afternoon in 1888, but it was sufficient to give the Rovers their first victory over the powerful Metropolitan side. James Southworth played magnificently in partnership with Forbes, who so distinguished himself that the committee unanimously came to the conclusion that he must change his place of residence. After some hesitation the Vale of Leven defender assented to the proposition. The following December "The Blackburn Times" announced that he had opened a hosiery and gentlemen's outfitting business, also that he "has already made himself at home." In those days Mr. Forbes was sometimes to be seen on the concert platform as a vocalist, on which occasions he was invariably encored. He still carries on his flourishing business, and is an honoured citizen in the town of his adoption.

Though North End were not in the same class when they originally met the Rovers, their improvement was so gratifying that in the first season of the League they carried off the championship without losing a match and won the English Cup without having a goal scored against them. That winter the "Invincibles" defeated the "Blue and Whites" at Deepdale (1–0), and drew at Blackburn (2–2). The previous season the sides had been in opposition on successive Saturdays, in the League and in the Lancashire Cup. When Preston won the first match by 4–3 it was believed by their supporters that they had "a bit up their sleeve," and that on the following Saturday they would play for all they were worth with the intention of winning by not fewer than three clear goals. On this assumption a large number of Prestonians came over to Blackburn, and lavishly backed their favourites. The result, though, was precisely the same as in the preceding game, which caused much wailing among the discomfited visitors.

By general consent the Rovers were a great team, but they did not always live up to their reputation. They had their "off days." The scribes who reported the matches were so conscientious that this is the sort of comment the old Rovers used to read in "The Blackburn Times" when they failed to do themselves justice (we purposely omit the names): "—— and —— played like duffers. They were as selfish as they could be with each other, and if they do not mend their manners the best thing the committee can do is to treat them as they have treated other sinners in this respect." On another occasion when the "Blue and Whites," at full strength,

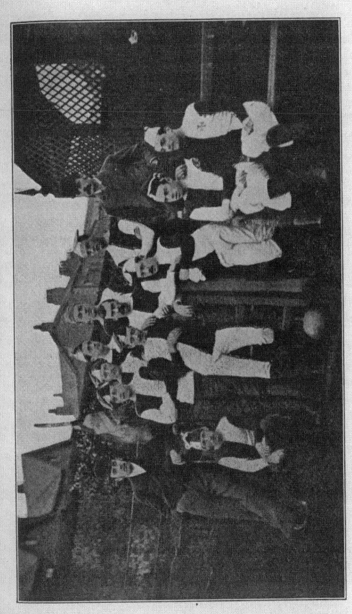

EARLY ROVERS.

BACK ROW: T. GREENWOOD, H. GREENWOOD. J. HAWORTH, ARTHUR THOMAS (IN CIVILIAN ATTIRE).
MIDDLE ROW: F. BIRTWISTLE, J. BALDWIN, J. DUCKWORTH, T. DEAN, R. BIRTWISTLE, J. LEWIS, F. HARGREAVES,
FRONT ROW: H. IBBOTSON (IN CIVILIAN ATTIRE), J. DUCKWORTH, T. DEAN, R. BIRTWISTLE, J. LEWIS, F. HARGREAVES,
W. DUCKWORTH.

were beaten 6–3 by Aston Villa, at Birmingham, the commentator said: "The Blackburn players evidently suffered from nerves, and at one period of the game rushed wildly about the field with little aim or combination."

Following an agitation by Lancashire clubs professionalism was legalised in England in July, 1885. This departure, which had far-reaching consequences, did not meet with the approval of such stalwarts as Dr. Morley, who regarded football as a recreation and deplored the introduction of the business element, for the benefit of professional players. About this time the Rovers had an unhappy experience at Manchester. In a match with Newton Heath, who were all imported professionals and big fellows, the "Blue and Whites" were knocked about like ninepins. Their science was unavailing against brute force. The Rovers lost 2–1, but it was conceded that physique and not skill had decided the issue. In fact, so secure a hold had professionalism already obtained that it was then forecasted that "the most successful team of the future will be the one that has the greatest amount of money at its back, and that can afford to pay for the finest talent in the land." Regret was expressed that the contests were no longer confined to sides representative of the best players that any town or district could produce, but that clubs were relying more and more on men drawn from all parts of the kingdom.

A curious incident is associated with a visit of Bolton Wanderers, in December, 1888. The Rovers started without Fecitt. A little later a substitute was found in Stothert, of the Bohemians, who, as related in the report of the game, "came reluctantly to the aid of the Rovers, and received anything but generous treatment from the spectators. Of course, he did not play as well as the other members of the home side, but seeing he came against his will to oblige the Rovers, the crowd might have accepted his efforts in a better spirit." At all events, this "unwilling substitute" rendered an important service by scoring the fourth and equalising goal for the "Blue and Whites."

The Rovers entered the 'nineties in gallant spirits, with a team reputed to be as strong as any in the palmy days of the past. It was not long, however, before they discovered that the impetus given to football by the League competition made greater demands on their skill and stamina than were required in ordinary club games. The absence of efficient reserves began to be acutely felt. When members of the premier side became stale through overwork or were incapacitated by injury most of the men who filled the temporary vacancies were unequal to the task imposed on them. An astute committee sought to repair this defect by importing new blood.

Hitherto the side had been principally composed of local players, but now the Scottish invasion commenced in real earnest. Incidentally, Lofthouse was welcomed back from Accrington, whither he had strayed; but the chief interest centred in the new men. Tom Brandon, then 20 years of age, was allured from Paisley St. Mirren. As he was one of the best backs in Scotland, his capture was accounted a master stroke, especially as James Southworth was not always able to accompany the team on long distance journeys. "Geordie" Dewar, who had graduated from a junior club to the famous Dumbarton team, was also obtained to occupy the centre-half position, though later he moved to right-half. Dewar, who was an upholsterer, had been capped by Scotland. His style was not particularly attractive, but exceedingly effective.

Another celebrity who linked his fortunes with the Rovers was Harry Campbell, also an international. He was a dyer by trade and a footballer by inclination. In Scotland to this day followers of football talk of the genius of McCallum and Campbell, who when with Renton formed one of the greatest wings in the history of the game and helped their club to win the Scottish Cup and the Glasgow Charity Cup. It used to be said that a partner or centre who could not shine when Campbell was alongside him ought to secure some other occupation as a means of livelihood.

As wing halves Dewar was supported on the left by the celebrated "Jimmy" Forrest, one of the grandest players ever connected with the club; and on the right, for a time, by Jimmy

JAMES H. FORREST.

Photo by Rudent, Blackburn

JOHN FORBES.

D. H. GREENWOOD.

H. ARTHUR.

Douglas, another splendid and popular veteran, whose marvellous form evoked unstinted admiration. Soon after Douglas gained international honours with Scotland he went to Barrow and then settled in Blackburn, in 1881, taking the place of R. Birtwistle at inside-right. Mr. Forrest, now a director of the Rovers' club, played for England at 19, and for a dozen years wore the blue and white jersey with distinction.

With such a powerful defence at their command and with tried and trusted players in the van, the Rovers' prospects seemed to be exceedingly bright. Soon, however, there was an outcry for a "first-class custodian." Appreciating the seriousness of the situation the committee spared no effort to solve the problem, though conspicuous success did not reward their zeal. That season (1889-90) no fewer than seven custodians kept watch and ward for the "Blue and Whites" —McOwen, Arthur, Doig, Wilkie, Paul, Lowe and Home.

Of these none received a more enthusiastic reception than the veteran "Herby" Arthur, who had joined the club as a right-half as far back as the season 1880-81. Soon afterwards he volunteered to fill a vacancy in goal for the second eleven, and revealed such aptitude that he was promptly retained in that position. Thus by an accident he found his true sphere, and laid the foundation of his brilliant career as a goalkeeper. As a lad he was in the ranks of King's Own, a local junior organisation, that also furnished the Rovers with such players as Forrest, Fecitt (a polished inside-left), Joe Sowerbutts, Lofthouse, A. Barton, and Bob Blenkhorn. On his third appearance with the seniors, in May, 1883, against Blackburn Olympic, in the final for the East Lancashire Charity Cup, which the "Blue and Whites" won 6-3, Arthur confirmed the excellent impression he had previously made. As a result he was given a permanent place in the first team.

On seven occasions he played for his country, twice representing England in the all-important encounter against Scotland; and made 13 appearances for Lancashire County. From time to time he was the central figure in remarkable exploits. Once he danced in a fog, and later treated a blizzard with contempt. Early in the second half of a game at Leamington-road, in December, 1888, Notts County enjoyed a lead of 2–0. Then a heavy fog enveloped the ground, and under cover of it the Rovers rattled up five goals in no time. At ten yards distance the ball was undiscernible. Arthur could not see what was happening. While his colleagues were peppering the Notts charge he was dancing about in the home goal, all eyes and ears and with arms poised ready to repel an attack. His duties that afternoon must have resembled a nightmare. The visitors appealed for the Rovers' goals to be disallowed because the fog was so dense that the referee could not actually see them scored, but this special pleading was in vain.

While the fog at Blackburn did the "Blue and Whites" a good turn, there was another occasion when it rendered them a distinct disservice. They had gone to Liverpool to play Everton, the president of which, Mr. John Holden, entertained some of the Blackburn officials and players prior to the game. The atmospheric conditions were so bad that the clubs agreed that the fixture should be classed as a friendly. On this clear understanding the elevens took the field. From the centre of the stand it was impossible to see either goalkeeper at the same time. The crowd on the far side were completely blotted out by the fog, their presence being indicated by the flaring of matches as smokers lit their pipes or cigarettes. Everton won. Both clubs went to the next meeting of the League in Manchester with a mutually arranged date for the replay. To the intense surprise of everybody the committee decided that the match must stand, the "Blue and Whites" thus losing two valuable points. Everton were in no way to blame, because they were just as astonished as the Rovers at the inexplicable action of the League.

Burnley was the scene of another incident with which Arthur's name will ever be associated. Snow was falling with blinding force when the Rovers arrived on the ground on December 12th, 1891, consequently they had doubts about the wisdom of playing. According to the referee's report to the Football League, they lodged no objection with him, and the match was commenced. In

JACK SOUTHWORTH.

EDGAR CHADWICK.

R. B. MIDDLETON.

W. DUCKWORTH.

the first 25 minutes Burnley registered three goals. At the interval when the teams had been absent ten minutes, during which there was considerable discussion among the Rovers as to whether they ought to resume, Mr. J. C. Clegg, of Sheffield, the referee, and now president of the Football Association, notified both sides that he would start the game in two minutes. He waited four and then gave the signal. At that time some of the "Blue and Whites" had not left the dressing-room.

Earlier on there had been friction between a player on each side, who had come to blows, and the second half had not been long in progress when they squared up again, whereupon both men received marching orders. This was the prelude to an extraordinary scene, culminating in the whole of the Rovers, except Arthur, leaving the field. As they refused to return Mr. Clegg directed Burnley to recommence the game, with the lone Blackburn custodian to set them at defiance—one man against eleven! In his predicament Arthur successfully claimed for offside, but dallied so long in taking the free kick that the referee applied the closure, the score standing at 3–0 in favour of Burnley. Old supporters yet refer with pride to the unquenchable courage of Mr. Arthur on that bitter and exciting day. The club subsequently apologised to the League for the team seeking shelter, advancing the explanation that the players were benumbed with the cold. The League expressed strong disapproval of their conduct in leaving the field without consulting the referee. Two days after this memorable match "Herby" Arthur was given a benefit, Sunderland providing the opposition. The Mayor (Mr. J. N. Boothman) attending in his official capacity, found himself in a new role on being asked to kick-off. His Worship, however, was quite equal to the occasion, for after divesting himself of his silk hat and overcoat he drove the ball at a spanking pace down the field.

Doig, from whom so much was expected, flitted like a shadow across the screen and then disappeared. Coming to the town from Arbroath on November 13th, 1889, he made his one and only appearance for the Rovers three days later, when he helped to defeat

Notts County 9–1 at Blackburn. A gem of a goalkeeper, his duties were very light, but smartly performed. Evidently the atmosphere did not suit him, because he immediately returned to Scotland. The next heard of him was that he had joined Sunderland. As he was the registered player of the Blackburn club the Wearsiders committed a breach of the regulations in signing him, but as the Rovers did not wish to cause trouble they consented to his transfer. Doig rendered meritorious service to Sunderland for 14 continuous seasons and later joined Liverpool.

It will be news to most people that, at an earlier period in their history, through the lamentable obtuseness of a scout the "Blue and Whites" lost another famous player in J. W. Crabtree. When he began his football career word reached Blackburn that he was a "likely lad." An emissary was sent to watch him. He returned with the report that the player was "no good." This judge of footballers was despatched on the same mission a second and even a third time, but he adhered to his opinion that Crabtree was "not a footballer and never would be!" If the club had been wise enough to change their scout they could have secured a versatile player, who, while with Burnley and Aston Villa, was capped on 14 occasions.

Blemishes in goalkeeping and a tendency to underestimate the capacity of opponents marred the Rovers' performances in the League competition in the season 1889-90. Nevertheless their record was an improvement on the previous winter, and the character of the victories stamped it as unmistakably superior. A heavy defeat (6–0) by Queen's Park, at Glasgow, was due to the fact that no fewer than six of the Rovers' regular players were engaged in international matches.

CHAPTER III. — "FIRST ASSOCIATION CLUB IN THE WORLD."

Opening of Ewood Park — Mr. Mitchell's Notable Captures — Old Warriors Make Their Bow — Burnley Pelted with Stones — Exorcising an Evil Spirit — Brandon "Barracked."

YOU have had many ups and downs, but today you occupy the proud position of being the first Association club in the world." This unsolicited testimonial to the Blackburn Rovers was furnished by Mr. W. Forrest, of Turton, then President of the Lancashire Association, at a dinner given by Dr. Morley to celebrate the opening of Ewood Park on September 13th, 1890. It was cordially endorsed by the other guests, who rejoiced that the old club had acquired such magnificent headquarters, with the possibility of a future that might even eclipse the fame of the past. Since then Ewood Park has been transformed into one of the finest enclosures in the country, with palatial stands, a beautiful board-room panelled in oak; ample accommodation for officials and players, a recreation room, and all the latest improvements that ingenuity can suggest. Thirty-five years ago it was estimated to comfortably hold 25,000 spectators; now it can house 65,000, though it has not been taxed to this extent, seeing that the biggest crowd it has yet contained numbered 60,011 on the occasion of the visit of Blackpool on March 7th last, in the fourth round of the Association Cup. On Xmas Day, 1921, 53,000 spectators were present at the League match with North End, and the following February there was an attendance of 45,249 at the Cup-tie with Huddersfield Town.

Except that once they had what might be termed a lovers' quarrel, the Rovers and Accrington had long been the best of friends, although keen antagonists. Therefore, it was appropriate that the "Reds" should have the honour of assisting at the opening of the new ground. The weather smiled on the auspicious event. Cheap bookings from Blackpool, Colne, Bury, Wigan, Manchester, Clitheroe and Liverpool brought hundreds of visitors eager to show their appreciation of the enterprise of the Blackburn club. Accrington, who had engaged more players than in any previous season, were represented by the following powerful eleven, which included several of their recent importations: Hay, McDermid (late of Sunderland Albion), Stephenson; Haworth, Sanders, Tattersall; Gallocher, Kirkham, Barbour, Thompson (St. Mirren), and Orr (Dumbarton). The home side was composed of Lowe; Brandon, Forbes; Barton, Dewar, Forrest; Townley, Walton, Southworth, Campbell, and Lofthouse. The game was of a pulsating character, and though the "Blue and Whites" had the better forward line they could not penetrate their opponents' defence. Indeed, a feature of the match was the almost faultless display given by Hay, McDermid and Stephenson. A very lively ball upset the calculations of some of the players. Still, if no goals were scored by either side, the spectators had plenty of thrills. Accrington returned home in high glee, proud of the fact that on this historic occasion they had shared the spoils with their valiant rivals.

After the match Dr. Morley, in replying to congratulations, confessed that he was getting old, but he added, "I am determined to keep my heart young. Football provides me with the only bit of relaxation I allow myself amid the cares and monotony of every-day life, and I will not willingly let it go." The same spirit animates thousands of people who in the great winter pastime seek distraction from "the cares that infest the day."

On learning that trouble had developed between Renton and the Scottish Association, the Blackburn committee, still engaged on the task of team building, promptly despatched their representatives to the north. They returned with Gow, the Renton

N. WALTON.

J. BROWN.

F. SUTER.

Photo by Lindsey, Darwen

W. A. McOwen.

goalkeeper, formerly with Vale of Leven, but he did not prove as reliable under the bar as Pennington, whose previous experience had been gained with south-west Lancashire clubs, by whom he was considered to be "second to none." Sunderland had good reason to remember Gow's first appearance at Ewood Park, because it was a bit of sharp practice on his part that prevented the visitors equalising. As the Scot could not get at a shot, he got out of the difficulty by bending the crossbar, the ball in consequence travelling over, instead of under. The Wearsiders, who were beaten 3–2. were incensed because the referee ignored their claim for a goal. Earlier the Rovers had been deprived of what they asserted was a legitimate point, hence it was felt that the new custodian had adroitly squared matters. The spectators were much amused at the incident, particularly as the visiting goalkeeper was none other than Doig, who had mysteriously vanished from Blackburn the season before, and was now making his debut at Ewood Park. To their intense satisfaction he was thrice beaten. Sunderland were in a very grumpy mood when time expired.

A crushing reverse inflicted by the County at Derby, when 13 goals were scored in a remarkable game, of which five were credited to the Rovers, almost faded into oblivion when the "Blue and Whites" twice defeated North End in League engagements, a feat that had not been previously accomplished by any club in one season. At Deepdale the "Invincibles" had lost 2–1, and three weeks later 20,000 spectators, at Blackburn, saw the Rovers emerge victorious from a punishing contest, in which they recorded the only goal of the match. Preston made a determined effort to rush their opponents off their feet, and nearly succeeded, for Pennington was quickly beaten, but the point was negatived by "hands." Then the home defence, recovering from the shock, played so superbly that their custodian did not handle more than three times. At the other end Trainer was kept busily employed fisting out shots, and once again demonstrated that he was "prince of goalkeepers." On the conclusion of the game the visitors were convinced that the Rovers had the finest halves and backs in the kingdom. Barton, Dewar and Forrest formed the intermediate line, with Brandon and Forbes behind them.

Like Forrest, Barton first saw the light in Blackburn, and was a prominent member of the Witton side before joining the Rovers. When his chance came with the seniors he showed that during his probation in the second eleven he had not allowed the grass to grow under his feet. With Forrest as his beau-ideal of a half-back, he had patterned his style on that of the older player, than whom he could not have had a better model. It was a real misfortune to the club when Barton's brilliant career was prematurely terminated by a twisted knee, sustained at Birmingham in September, 1891. Before then he had won county and international honours, as well as two F.A. Cup medals.

It was in the first season at Ewood Park that the widely-discussed boycott of an international occurred. The Football Association paid the club an undoubted compliment by selecting the new ground for the great contest of the year, England v. Scotland, and then aroused a storm of criticism by choosing a side that did not contain a single Rover. So bitter was the indignation felt by local football followers that they deprived themselves of the rare pleasure of witnessing the chief representative game of the season. Not more than 6,000 spectators gathered in the spacious enclosure, the receipts being a paltry £334. That the action of the Selection Committee in overlooking the claims of such talented players as Southworth and Barton did not meet with general approval, was evidenced by a comment of the "Athletic News" that their exclusion was "not only an injustice to the men themselves, but an injustice to England." Curiously enough the star artistes for England were Edgar Chadwick and Johnny Holt, then with Everton, and both natives of Blackburn. Of the five internationals that have been decided at Blackburn it is singular that this is the only one in which England gained the verdict. Scotland had previously beaten them here, while Wales, in three visits (the last in March, 1924), won the first and third matches and drew the second.

Local resentment at the Selection Committee gave place to satisfaction when Jack Southworth was awarded his third cap the following April (1892), this time against Scotland, at Glasgow, when England prevailed by 4–1. The victorious eleven included four Blackburn-born men— Southworth, Holt, Chadwick, and Reynolds (then with West Bromwich Albion, and later a shining light of Aston Villa). The last-named player had the distinction of appearing for two countries in Association international matches. While living in the Emerald Isle he played for Ireland. Subsequently it was ascertained that he was born in Blackburn, of Irish parents. As birth qualification is the governing factor England, therefore, had the call on his services, and honoured him on eight occasions.

Of the many additions to the playing staff in the 'nineties, burly Johnny Murray, late of Sunderland and Vale of Leven, was a notable acquisition. Occasionally he figured at half-back, but is better remembered for his fine displays at full-back in partnership with Forbes or Brandon, while it is interesting to recall that Nat. Walton, who had been a member of the side since the early 'eighties and could play equally well in almost any position, gave further proof of his versatility by succeeding Pennington in goal in 1892-3. The next season he transferred his services to Nelson. In Adam Ogilvie, who filled the vacancy, a solution was found to a problem that had long baffled the committee. Among the famous triumvirates connected with the Rovers not the least celebrated was that of "Ogilvie, goal; Brandon and Murray, backs." They distinguished themselves on many a hard-fought field. Before these three became associated, however, Brandon had wandered away to Sheffield for a couple of seasons, but he fell out with the Wednesday, joined Nelson, with whom he played against the "Blue and Whites," and then wished to return to Blackburn. Sheffield, though, declined to transfer him, but after much wrangling and negotiation they were finally induced to withdraw their opposition.

Mr. T. B. Mitchell, then secretary of the club, added to his laurels when in October, 1892, he captured Geordie Anderson, captain of Leith Athletic, and Harry Marshall, of the Heart of Midlothian. On the 29th of the same month what became a classic half-back line—Dewar, Anderson, and Marshall—was first seen at Ewood Park. Walton was in goal, Murray and Forbes were the backs, and the attack consisted of Mann (East Stirlingshire), Sawers, Southworth (soon to be transferred to Everton for what was described as the "handsome" amount of £400), Hall, and Bowdler. North End were the visitors. Despite a pitiless downpour of rain thousands of spectators witnessed a stubborn contest that ended in a draw (0–0). So splendidly did the "Blue and Whites" acquit themselves that in the second half they completely broke up the combination of the famous Preston forwards, who had to bow to the superiority of Blackburn's new half-back line.

Famous lights of other days appeared at Ewood Park in March, 1892, on the occasion of a match for the benefit of a gentleman who had been an enthusiastic supporter of Blackburn Olympic. With the generosity for which they have ever been noted, the committee readily granted the use of the ground, and as there was a large attendance the beneficiare reaped a substantial sum. For the most part the teams were composed of veterans who had served with distinction in the ranks of the Olympic and the Rovers. These old warriors were acclaimed by many spectators with vivid memories of their exploits in bygone years. The "Blue and Whites" suffered defeat by the odd goal in three, and the success of their former rivals was popular with the crowd, who had not forgotten that Olympic were the first provincial team to win the Association Cup, in 1883, beating the Old Etonians 2–1, after an extra half-hour. Mr. T. Hacking, who kept goal for them in that celebrated contest, again donned the jersey at Ewood Park in March, 1892, giving an exhibition that was a revelation to those who had not previously seen him in action.

At one time football partisans whose zeal outran their discretion were in the habit of relieving their feelings by pelting opponents with stones and mud. It was great sport while it lasted,

J. K. HORNE.
H. FECITT.

W. DAVIES.
W. TOWNLEY.

though those foolish enough to indulge in it had scant regard for the trouble it might cause. For example, when Burnley were here in December, 1892, they complained of the liveliness of their journey to the railway station. They had lost an exciting match by 2–0. In the last few minutes the referee had found it necessary to order a player on each side to leave the field. Rightly or wrongly, a section of the crowd believed that the visitors were to blame for what had happened. As a sequel, Burnley alleged that they were bombarded with missiles as they drove in a wagonette along Bolton-road. Jack Hillman, their goalkeeper, was reported to have been struck in the face by a stone, and the players generally were said to have had narrow escapes from injury. When the matter was investigated by a commission of the Football Association the Rovers' club put in affidavits to the effect that there was no stone-throwing within at least 200 yards of Ewood Park, and that as far as they knew nothing of the kind took place even at that distance. The club were honourably acquitted, the commission dismissing the appeal and holding that no blame attached to the Rovers' committee. They suggested, however, that it would have been more prudent if protection had been provided for the Burnley team until they reached the town. As the complainants had asked not for a penalty, but for a ruling on the subject, they were probably equally satisfied with the decision.

Hereabouts the "Blue and Whites" were performing only moderately in the League. In the early part of the season 1892-3 they did not win a game for 10 weary weeks. Their supporters were almost in despair. Then, however, Dewar, Anderson and Marshall were incorporated as the half-back line. That masterly stroke effected an immediate improvement. In the end 29 points were collected, the most so far obtained, and the side won their way to the semi-final of the national cup competition.

After hope had been deferred so often in the League tourney, the Rovers redeemed themselves in the presence of 28,000 spectators by inflicting a decisive defeat on Sunderland in the third round of the Association Cup, on February 18th, 1893.

Incidentally, there was a record gate of £760, the previous best being £454. Those figures have long gone by the board, and appear utterly insignificant when compared with the £3,396 taken when Huddersfield Town were at Blackburn in the Cup competition in February, 1922, and with the £4,482 drawn from the Cup-tie with Blackpool in March last. Never was a victory more welcome than that against Sunderland. When the "Blue and Whites" scored against the breeze and with the rain in their faces there was great cheering, but when two more goals were registered after the interval the delight of the spectators knew no bounds, and when the whistle blew (according to the scribes of the day), "cheer after cheer rang through the valley." The home side played with the utmost confidence, their halves particularly excelling. Entranced by this achievement a jubilant supporter addressed the following post-card to the Press: "Southworth is the finest centre-forward and Anderson the finest half-back the world has ever seen, or ever will have the luck to see. Blackburn Rovers have never won a League match for the last three years without Southworth—the only match they won playing without him being that against Chester last season." The Cestrians, by the way, were beaten 6–1.

The optimists found cause for satisfaction in the next season (1893-4). Some splendid successes were chronicled, chiefly by the aid of improved marksmanship, and the club finished fourth in the League. While the Rovers scored 148 goals their defence capitulated on but 96 occasions. The team played admirably on their own ground, but were by no means as formidable on tour. It is singular that in four of their five most emphatic victories they piled up five or more goals, and that in their five heaviest reverses they sacrificed five or more goals.

It was at this period that Harry Chippendale and Jimmy Whitehead formed a right wing that gained international honours, and that in many matches was invincible. Tall and well-built, Chippendale was no stranger to the team, as he had been a member for at least two seasons. A fast and forcing player, he finished dashing runs with accurate shots or centres, and was certainly a live wire. Whitehead, who had been capped while with Accrington, was a debutant at Ewood. Compared with his partner, he was short and stocky, but he tackled the biggest backs with a zest that was refreshing. Crafty and skilful, he often toyed with opponents, and sometimes stood head and shoulders over his colleagues. He was such a powerful shot that with one of his drives he knocked Rowley, the Stoke custodian, clean into the net at Blackburn. Much satisfaction was felt locally when this talented pair were selected as England's right wing against Ireland, at Belfast, in March. 1894, the game ending 2–2. Both men gave a good account of themselves, and Whitehead had the pleasure of scoring one of England's goals.

The Rovers' left wing included yet another famous Blackburn footballer in Jimmy Haydock, an assistant master at Furthergate School. His initial appearance with the League eleven was against Wolverhampton Wanderers, on September 27th, 1890, and the following year he superseded Lofthouse against Notts County at Trent Bridge. By then he had developed into a smart forward, and he continued to render brilliant service to the club until ill-health compelled his retirement from the game in 1897. To the deep regret of a wide circle of friends, Mr. Haydock passed away on March 24th, 1900, at the early age of 27. At different times he filled each of the forward positions, his favourite berth being outside right, to which he was drafted in 1894, on Chippendale being transferred to his correct position at outside-left. Haydock and Whitehead quickly understood each other's methods, were adepts at short passing, and were so skilful that they frequently made rings round the best defenders. The Furthergate teacher had a remarkable experience against Liverpool in the first match that the latter played as members of the First Division, for no fewer than seven of his shots struck the bar or the uprights. Even if he did not always find the mark this plucky and determined player was never afraid of firing at goal. In 1895 he was chosen for England against Ireland, but, unfortunately, indisposition kept him out of the field.

"Horses for courses" is a well-known racing aphorism. This maxim is equally applicable to football. In the case of the Rovers it took them 12 years to break the spell that bewitched them when they visited the Wanderers at Bolton. During the whole of that period they could not register a victory at the headquarters of their Lancashire opponents. When success came at last it had a curious origin. Being without a fixture for the final Saturday of the season in 1894, the "Blue and Whites" hastily arranged a meeting with Bolton, and won 4–0, at Pike-lane. In that way the evil spirit was exorcised.

Earlier in the year Tom Brandon, in a League game against United at Sheffield, was made the object of a hostile demonstration by a section of the crowd, who had a rod in pickle for him in consequence of his refusal to play for the Wednesday. On making his appearance he was roundly hooted. This conduct continued right up to the interval. Every time Brandon touched the ball irate spectators gave vent to their spleen. As the players trooped off at half-time some of the rougher element in the crowd assumed a threatening attitude. A stone was hurled at the famous back, and attempts were made to strike him. Such reprehensible behaviour aroused the indignation of the Rovers' officials, who took measures to prevent the further molestation of their men. The barracking, however, continued, and no one was sorry when the "Blue and Whites" were safely on their way home.

On the evening of October 20th, 1894, the Blackburn Rovers were the talk of the sporting world, because they had terminated a series of dazzling victories by Everton, who had won eight matches off the reel. There was not a dull moment in the whole ninety minutes of the game. "Geordie" Anderson covered himself with glory that afternoon. Jack Southworth led the Everton van, It was anticipated that there would be a rare duel between the brilliant centre-forward and the accomplished centre-half. As events showed Anderson proved himself a veritable Sherlock Holmes by the artfulness with which he checkmated his doughty opponent, whom he shadowed so effectively that Southworth's elusiveness

Sir William Coddington, Bart.

Photo by Davey & Sons, Harrogate

Sir John Rutherford, Bart.

Photo by Jerome, St. Annes

T. B. Mitchell.

C. F. Critchley.

and skill counted for next to nothing. The "Blue and Whites" won by 4–3, though the score was not a true index of the relative strength of the elevens, as impartial judges freely admitted that the winners were by far the better side. On that memorable occasion the Rovers did honour to themselves, the club and the town.

CHAPTER IV. — TOWN'S HOMAGE TO OLD CLUB.

Players Sacrifice a Week's Wages — Mr. Mitchell's Adventures — Seven Centre Forwards — Startling Accident to Spectators at Ewood Park — Stranded on Railway: Humours of an All-Night Vigil — Lancashire Cup Returns to Blackburn.

PUBLIC men of all shades of opinion and sportsmen whose names are still household words paid homage to the old club at the great bazaar held in the Exchange Hall early in 1895. Some who took a prominent part had not attained the dignities afterwards conferred on them, but we purposely use the titles by which they are now known. The appeal was for £1,500 to help liquidate the deficit caused by the transference of the headquarters from Leamington-road to Ewood Park. That removal cost £2,700. In response to this request for funds, £1,480 was raised, the net proceeds being £1,200. Mr. John Lewis discharged the duties of chairman of the bazaar committee, and Alderman C. F. Critchley, now Mayor of Lytham St. Annes, was the honorary secretary for the event. With the veteran Dr. Morley as his chairman, Sir Wm. Coddington, Bart., in performing the opening ceremony, recalled that he had always kept himself in touch with the affairs of the club, and had had occasion to refer to the Rovers in that august assembly, the House of Commons, while as president he was once served with a writ arising out of a dispute between the Blackburn club and one at Nottingham, but, happily, that affair went no further.

Others who filled leading roles on the subsequent days included Sir Edwin Hamer, who deputised for a vice-president in Sir W. H. Hornby, Bart.; Alderman A. Nuttall, who appeared in place of Mr. R. A. Yerburgh, unavoidably absent; the Mayor (Alderman R. T. Eastwood); Sir John Rutherford, Bart., a vice-president and an old playing member of the "Blue and Whites"; Alderman T. E. Thompson, another vice-president and nephew of Alderman W. Thompson; and Alderman J. N. Boothman, also a vice-president, who during his Mayoralty kicked off at "Herby" Arthur's benefit match at Ewood Park. Sir W. H. Hornby's absence, due to the illness of Lady Hornby, was deeply regretted, because he had ever been a generous patron of athletics, and, as Sir Edwin Hamer pointed out, "Blackburn sport and the name of Hornby are indissolubly linked." Emphasis was laid on the fact that by their magnificent performances on the field the Rovers had made the town known throughout the kingdom. The speakers might truthfully have gone a step further and said throughout the world. Among the distinguished guests special recognition was accorded Major Marindin. of the Royal Engineers, who refereed seven final ties for the Association Cup, a record that is not likely to be effaced.

The players, on their own initiative, generously subscribed a week's wages to the bazaar fund, it was a gracious act, testifying to the good feeling that prevailed between employers and employed. Mr. Harry Campbell, who presided over the meeting at which the players unanimously decided to contribute, subsequently received the following letter from Mr. Critchley: "I am instructed by the bazaar committee to express their deep appreciation of the kindness of the Rovers' players in sacrificing (for the bazaar fund) a week's salary. Between the officials of the Rovers' club and the players there has always existed the most cordial relations, and the spontaneous generosity alluded to is alike creditable to the players themselves and to the club in which they have shown so kindly an interest. It is, indeed, an example to the athletic world, and the best proof that (in spite of occasional and minor disputes, which must inevitably occur) the interests of the professional footballer and the officials of a club are identical. We thank each one of you very heartily for your generosity."

A popular and hard-working member of the bazaar committee was Mr. T. B. Mitchell, who for a long period was an important figure in the football world. A native of Kirkmahoe, Dumfries, he came to Blackburn about 1867, and from its inception took the keenest interest in the Rovers' club. Years before he became officially connected with it as secretary, he accompanied the team all over the country, and was an enthusiast of enthusiasts. Mr. Mitchell was a prime mover in the establishment of the Football League. A noted referee, he had the distinction of being the first to officiate at games in the four countries—England, Ireland, Scotland and Wales. Among his engagements were an international match at Glasgow, two final ties in the Irish Division of the Association Cup competition when clubs other than those in England and Wales were allowed to enter; and a final for the Welsh Cup. Fond of all kinds of sport, Mr. Mitchell was a dead shot with a gun, and as an owner of greyhounds met with more than average success at club meetings. On his appointment as secretary, a position he held about 12 years, he gave whole-hearted service to the club, which during his regime twice carried off the Association Cup. He resigned in October, 1896, but at the request of the committee did not immediately vacate office.

To Mr. Mitchell adventure was as the wine of life. In journeys across the Border in search of talented players, he was responsible for many brilliant coups, his captures including Forbes, Brandon, Dewar, Campbell, Gow, Anderson, and Marshall. The fact that he hailed from the Land o' Cakes was of inestimable value to him in these forays. At that time the transfer system did not exist, and the quests had to be conducted with the utmost secrecy, because the Scots, annoyed at the constant decoying of their clever players, did not stand on ceremony when they found an agent in their midst. During Mr. Mitchell's absence on one of these expeditions alarming rumours were circulated in Blackburn. It was reported that Highland followers of the game had discovered his presence, had chased him up hill and down dale, and that for his own safety the police had taken him into custody. A thrilling story was soon gathering moss, and developments were anxiously awaited. Afterwards it transpired that a local newspaper man had been beautifully hoaxed! Luckily, when the secretary heard of the affair he proved a good sport. Later he revealed the whole of the circumstances connected with that exciting trip. From the Rovers' standpoint Mr. Mitchell's mission had been quite as successful as on former occasions. It was true, though, that the natives had become aware of his purpose and that he had to exercise considerable caution and judgment in the performance of his duties. There was, however, no clashing with the police, although there might have been if clever strategy had not been employed. What happened was that the Blackburn secretary had a long scurry through a wild country district, negotiating hedges, walls, ditches and other obstacles which impeded his progress. As a result his clothes were badly torn. Eventually he sought sanctuary at a hotel, where he remained hidden for a few hours while a tailor hurriedly made him a new pair of trousers. Then he quietly boarded the next train southward, highly elated because he had secured yet another jewel to adorn the Rovers' crown.

Behind a somewhat stern exterior he hid a kindly nature. "What do you fellows want?" he angrily demanded of a party of Pressmen who called on him for information not yet released for publication. "Ten pounds a week and a soft job as a football club secretary!" daringly replied one of the visitors. "T.B." raged for a few minutes, and then, his wrath dissolving in a smile, he gave the required information. In his 78th year Mr. Mitchell passed away on the last Saturday in August, 1921, and was interred at the Blackburn cemetery. In addition to relatives, tributes of respect were paid by many of his former football associates, and the bearers were Messrs. J. Forbes, J. Forrest, N. Walton, and H. Fecitt, four old players who had earned distinction with the "Blue and Whites."

Though they had raised a substantial sum, which placed the club's finances in a healthy condition, the committee's troubles

SEASON 1894-95.

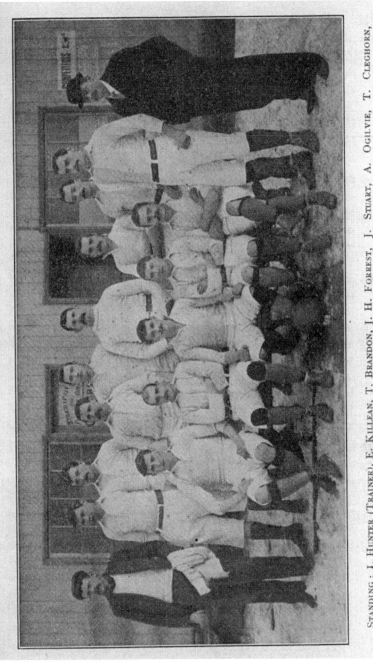

STANDING : J. HUNTER (TRAINER), E. KILLEAN, T. BRANDON, J. H. FORREST, J. STUART, A. OGILVIE, T. CLEGHORN,
G. DEWAR, J. MURRAY, H. CAMPBELL.
SITTING : P. GORDON, J. SORLEY, G. ANDERSON, JOS. HARGREAVES, H. CHIPPENDALE.

were not ended. They wanted better results from the team. The players were clever individually, but the forwards as a file did not give complete satisfaction. It was no easy task finding a leader comparable with Jack Southworth. At least seven men were tried, with more or less success. In the hope of evolving what is commonly called a "match-winning attack" the committee resorted to various reshuffling experiments. But these constant changes, far from producing the results required, had an unsettling effect on the line, and it was some time before cohesion was attained. Jos. Hargreaves, Calvey, Teddie Killean, Stuart, of Coathbridge, Sorley, of Middlesbrough, Turnbull, of Burnley, and Tierney, of Chorley, all operated at centre-forward within three seasons.

Killean, regarded as the hope of his side, had plenty of football in him. With style and speed, he could furnish colleagues with accurate passes, even when he was hampered by opponents, and could generally give half-backs a run for their money. In September, 1894, it was felt that he would fill the vacancy caused by Southworth's absence. As a leader, however, he was not in the first flight, and was moved to inside-left, his favourite forward position, where he performed so successfully that the following year he was hailed as the most improved member of the Rovers' attack. It was then predicted that he would make a name for himself as an inside-left. His prospects, though, were adversely affected by his mercurial temperament, which caused him to indulge in fancy tricks, such as practising the hornpipe on the ball instead of shooting at goal. Later he developed into a sound defender.

For a time Stuart lived up to his reputation, but then fell away, and Jos. Hargreaves, restored to the leadership, did valiant service, despite his lack of inches. Turnbull, signed in March, 1895, at a transfer fee of £75, could fill any of the inside positions. Engaged primarily as a centre-forward, he knew how to control a ball and was a goal-getter. When with the Ewood side he was sometimes more confident at inside-left than at centre-forward. Turnbull gave a fine exhibition in the match with Everton on New Year's Day, 1896. During this game Anderson was hurt and Chippendale went centre-half. When the excitement was at its height, with both teams struggling hard for mastery, a section of the switch-back stand at the north end of the ground collapsed without the slightest warning. Five spectators were injured. Naturally, this untoward occurrence caused some confusion, especially as a portion of the crowd swarmed over the rails into the arena, but the police soon restored order. Everton won 3–2. Still, if the "Blue and Whites" had received their deserts the visitors' third point would have been disallowed for offside. Haydock headed the Rovers' first goal, from a grand centre by Chippendale, and the second was one of the finest ever seen on a football ground, Haydock rousing 20,000 spectators to great enthusiasm by a brilliant run, in which he defeated four opponents, and then transferred to Turnbull, who converted. That afternoon the Furthergate school teacher played magnificently.

That the "Blue and Whites" enjoyed a well-deserved reputation for skill and tenacity was reflected by a comment in "Pastime," a sporting journal, the Editor of which assured his readers that "Blackburn Rovers and West Bromwich Albion are the free-lances of the League, and it is never safe to count on beating them."

It must be rare indeed for a football team to find itself stranded overnight on the railway in consequence of imperfect communications between rival companies' services, but such was the experience of the Rovers on one occasion when they visited Sunderland in the 'nineties. Starting for Blackburn by the earliest possible train after the match, they arrived at Normanton, near Wakefield, to discover that the last train for East Lancashire had just gone. The Rovers' saloon was detached and run into a bay. At first the players and a Pressman who accompanied them on that week-end journey made light of the situation. With Mr. T. B. Mitchell, secretary, they proceeded to the principal hotel in the neighbourhood with the object of obtaining sleeping accommodation. Their spirits were somewhat damped when they learned that there was a "full house," and that no beds were available. Inquiries in other quarters met with the same result. Consequently the party retraced their steps to Normanton railway station, with the dismal prospect of spending the night in the saloon – a matter of something approaching 12 hours before the journey home could be resumed. It was a cheerless and tedious business. Many wiled away the time by playing cards; now and again a player would "go nap" in a sitting position in a corner of the compartment, or stretch himself full length on the seat, risking an occasional jest as the penalty for a snore, the louder the snore the merrier the jest. "Forty winks" served a useful purpose, after which one or other would take a stroll down the uncovered platform, the fresh morning air as light began to dawn imparting some charm to the long wait. At length the dreary vigil came to an end. All were glad when the saloon was once more coupled up. Blackburn, however, was not reached until about Sunday noon. Happily, none of the party felt any the worse for the unusual experience. The only atoning feature of the adventure was that the "inner man" was not allowed to suffer.

While the season 1894-5 left much to be desired, the drabness was relieved by gleams of brightness. The side's form fluctuated considerably. In some games the Rovers were irresistible; in others they almost touched zero. Constant remodelling of the attack militated against success, but the defence was not disturbed to the same extent. The fact remains, however, that for the second season in succession the results on foreign soil were very unsatisfactory, only two League victories being recorded away from home, against Bolton Wanderers and Nottingham Forest.

Marshall's disablement in an East Lancashire Charity Cup tie with Burnley in September was an early and costly misfortune, as it dissolved the renowned half-back line that had previously been such a source of strength. He returned to his home at Portobello, where he followed his occupation as a boatman. At that time it was believed that Marshall would be incapable of playing football again. However, in 1896, he was able to assist his old club—Heart of Midlothian—in a Scottish League game against St. Bernard.

Dewar was also unlucky in regard to injuries. At this juncture Jimmy Forrest, who had practically decided to retire, gallantly came to the rescue. In all parts of the country the veteran won the admiration of spectators by his clever and finished exhibitions. In the past he had tendered magnificent service; now, when the club was in a real difficulty, he responded nobly to the call. The gap caused by Marshall's absence was worthily filled by Tommy Cleghorn, formerly of Leith, a great-little player who never knew when he was beaten. He worked like a demon, tackled effectively, and headed the ball with wonderful skill. His value was enhanced by the judgment he displayed in feeding the forwards. On many occasions Cleghorn roused crowds to a frenzy of enthusiasm.

One of the tit-bits of the campaign was a brilliant victory over Small Heath, who were vanquished 9–1 at Ewood Park in the New Year. In the first half the "Blue and Whites" scored thrice, and on changing ends ran away with their Midland opponents. Through a defender being injured, the visitors resorted to the one-back game, a policy attended with disastrous consequences to themselves, for the home forwards, adapting their moves to the altered circumstances, simply riddled the defence. Killean, as an inside forward, left his impress on the game, and Chippendale was in his happiest mood, his centres being remarkable for their accuracy. A week later the Rovers appeared at Turf Moor, a name that supplied Blackburn critics with material for ironical comments, inasmuch as there was hardly a particle of turf to be seen on the ground, which resembled a typical sandhill. On this "sward" Burnley defeated their East Lancashire rivals by the odd goal in three. The "Blue and Whites," though, scarcely deserved such a fate. They attacked persistently, and were so much in evidence that Brandon and Forrest were popping at goal from the half-way line, but all their efforts failed to produce an equaliser.

In the same month Darwen cherished the hope that they would dismiss the Rovers from the Lancashire Senior Cup competition. Their players were very confident when they stepped on to Ewood Park, and their followers were elated when Ogilvie

J. Murray.

T. Brandon.

G. Anderson.

J. Haydock.

was beaten by King's clever shot. The home side, however, were not disheartened by this setback. On the contrary, they applied themselves to their task with greater earnestness, played beautiful football, gave Briggs, the Darwen custodian, the busiest afternoon he had experienced for a long time, and won comfortably by 4–1. Ogilvie had Brandon and Murray in front of him, while Forrest, Anderson and Cleghorn lent admirable support to Gordon, Whitehead, Sorley, Haydock and Chippendale. Forrest's exhibition was so skilful and resourceful that it challenged comparison with his superb displays at the zenith of his fame. Haydock, who was the pick of the forwards, sparkled like a diamond in the sun. His dribbling, feinting and shooting kept the Darwen rearguard on tenterhooks. Once he completely mystified his opponents by a brilliant solo effort, crowned by a glorious goal. Remembering their expectations, Darwen were crestfallen by the turn of events; their early goal proved to be merely a flash in the pan. About this time the Rovers' management were not exempt from criticism for installing Paddy Gordon, of Liverpool, at outside-right, thus severing the Haydock-Whitehead combination that had been so successful in the past.

Some fresh faces were seen at Ewood Park the following season, but the only distinct acquisition was Wilkie, of Partick Thistle, who performed meritoriously at inside-left. The great conundrum in the football world was whether the Rovers would improve and carry off the League championship? Certainly they started in a manner that enchanted their admirers. From the first six games they gathered nine points, represented by four wins and a draw. Unfortunately, as the tournament advanced this high standard was not maintained. For the want of an odd goal many matches were lost. Lack of finishing power told its tale. When the results were tabulated it was found that the club had dropped from the fifth to the seventh place in the table, that 12 games had been won, 13 lost, and 5 drawn. Against 40 goals obtained by the "Blue and Whites" their opponents scored 50. Considering the promise with which the season opened, the final record was anything but flattering.

It was in this season that the Rovers first measured their
League strength with Bury, promoted from the Second Division.
The debutants created a sensation by the way in which they tackled
the "Blue and Whites." When the pair met at Gigg-lane, on a bleak
day in December, Bury went off at a terrific pace on an ice-bound
ground. The Rovers, not properly shod for the treacherous surface,
sprawled about in all directions. It seemed, indeed, that nothing
could save them from defeat, for the home side not only gained
the lead, but played with such assurance that it was momentarily
expected that they would increase their score. Apart from the
one lapse, however, that trusty triumvirate, Ogilvie, Brandon and
Murray, succeeded in keeping the invaders at bay. Then salvation
came in the form of a fog, which caused the game to be abandoned
at the interval.

Early in the New Year the return fixture, this time, of
course, at Blackburn, aroused unusual interest. It was confidently
anticipated that the "Babes in the Wood" would be put to
sleep. To the consternation of the habitues of Ewood Park their
favourites were beaten 2–0. Prior to then, Bury had lost 11 of
their 17 engagements. But they had dauntless hearts, and their
pluck no less than their skill carried them to victory. Strive as they
would, the "Blue and Whites" could not turn the scale. Wilkie
made great efforts to pierce the opposing defence, but received
little support, except from Haydock. Brandon was so annoyed at
the feeble shooting that he joined the front line in the hope of
saving a point, at least. His marksmanship, though, was no better
than that of his colleagues. After this unexpected debacle the
crowd wended their way home in a dispirited mood. In March the
sides again encountered each other in the final for the Lancashire
Senior Cup, the contest being staged at Bolton. A hard game
saw each eleven score once, but in the April replay the Rovers
deservedly triumphed by 2–0. Thus, after the lapse of 11 years,
the county trophy returned to Blackburn, and there was much
rejoicing over the achievement. Seven days later Bury had their
revenge by defeating the Ewood representatives 2–0 at Gigg Lane

in the postponed League fixture. In these five events, in which they scored six goals to three, the promoted club plainly intimated that they were in congenial company in the higher circle, where, in fact, they remained for 17 years.

At the close of the campaign "The Blackburn Times" announced that Johnny Murray contemplated retiring and intended to apply for reinstatement as an amateur. For four seasons he had been a tower of strength to the side. Preferment at the hands of his employers was the sole reason for his decision, and he carried with him the best wishes of a wide circle of friends.

The insatiable appetite of the sporting public for football news was partly appeased by the activities of local journalists in the autumn of 1896. They kept the telegraph wires humming with the latest information about the "Blue and Whites," several of whom sustained nasty accidents in the trial matches, and when that kind of "copy" became exhausted the Pressmen spun racy yarns about the supposed idiosyncrasies of certain of the players. The stories tickled the palates of newspaper readers with the exception of a gentleman in Liverpool, who sent the following satirical letter to the Press: "If the Blackburn Rovers are not quite so famous as they were in the days when they had only to walk on to the football field and carry away the English Cup, the enterprising penny-a-liners of Blackburn are determined to provide the necessary excuses or keep them up to the scratch in the eyes of the great British public. The 1st of September had not dawned when our little world was startled with four full-backs out of five practically settled for the season. Then a centre-forward broke his collar bone, but recovered with remarkable speed, while a new full-back had the misfortune to wrench his knee. Then there was a player who would not sign. According to the correspondents, the success of the club depended on this circumstance, so the gentleman referred to said he'd play! Later telegrams contained news of more injured players, another gets married, and wires are scattered broadcast about a man being compelled to leave the field at Burnley because he was charged! Despite all this, the Rovers went on winning with wonderful

SEASON 1897-98.

STANDING : T. BRANDON, T. BOOTH, A. KNOWLES, E. KILLEAN, J. GLOVER, A. E. HOULKER.
SITTING : J. J. BRADBURY, H. GARSTANG, J. PROUDFOOT, J. WILKIE, J. CAMPBELL.

consistency, to the chagrin of the Blackburn scribes. While the craze lasts the team can be expected to have a real good time; and we may look forward to seeing such headlines as " 'Dewar and his Moustache,' 'Ogilvie's Sore Toe,' and 'Brandon Catches Cold!' "

CHAPTER V. — PESSIMISTS CONFOUNDED.

Committee Lecture Players — Six Goals Disallowed In One Match — Comical Incident at Wolverhampton — Dr. Morley and the Viscount — W. A. McOwen: A Football Prodigy.

In referring to the Rovers' prospects for the ensuing campaign, a commentator in "The Blackburn Times," in August, 1896, lamented that "the team is smaller than ever." Whether the stature of the players had anything to do with the matter or not, the side had a disastrous season, though, as a satirical writer at Liverpool observed, the "Blue and Whites" confounded the pessimists by the excellent account they gave of themselves in the first eight matches. Subsequently some of the men were irregular in their training. Hence it transpired in November that "this week the Rovers' players have appeared before the committee. They were given a quiet lecture on due attention being paid to training. A few players have been somewhat lax in putting in an appearance at the ground, where they are expected to go through a course of exercise. They have now been informed that proper attention will have to be paid to training and will be required to visit the ground every morning and afternoon. Any player who does not conform to orders will be severely dealt with."

This heart-to-heart talk had a salutary effect for the time being. Afterwards some of the men had a relapse. Alluding to this aspect "The Blackburn Times" reviewer asserted that the committee had "not been as strict as they might have been." Sixteen of the 30 League matches were lost, 11 were won, and the other three drawn. Finishing with 25 points, the Rovers were third from the bottom of the table, which was not surprising seeing that their goals numbered but 35, compared with 62 credited to opponents.

Among the recruits were Campbell, who was Wilkie's partner when with Partick Thistle, from which club Proudfoot was signed in February, 1897; Joy, a Preston North End custodian; A. Blackburn, of Mellor, a big, strapping full-back, brother of Fred Blackburn, who joined the club subsequently and as a forward gained international honours; and Tom Booth, of Ashton North End, who developed into a splendid half-back.

Walter Porter, another capable defender, had seen service with Mellor and St. John's before becoming a playing member of the Rovers, with whom he remained for two seasons. In the first (1895-6) he assisted the premier eleven in five League matches at left back. Except that he was kept out of the field for a short period by two accidents, he regularly donned the blue and white jersey the following winter. When Porter appeared in his second League game, against Bury, Jimmy Haydock gave him a useful tip by reminding him that Barbour, latterly a fullback, had been transferred to centre-forward in the hope of giving greater "punch" to the Bury attack. Soon after the kick-off, Porter and Barbour came into violent contact. The Rover, though, was prepared for the emergency, thanks to Haydock's warning. As his antagonist rushed at him, he braced himself for the charge, and the opposing centre-forward bounced off him. Immediately afterwards Barbour remarked to another Rover, "Who the dickens is that young fellow? He is as hard as nails!" The Blackburn left-back gave a fine display on that occasion. With a view to popularising Association football in a Rugby stronghold, the Rovers and North End played an exhibition game at Halifax. Brandon and Porter were the Blackburn backs. A heavy fog enveloped the ground, which made it difficult for the spectators to follow the proceedings. The teams, however, retained pleasant recollections of the visit, for they were warmly welcomed and hospitably entertained. Walter Porter's next appearance on the Halifax ground was when he and Tierney had the honour of playing for Lancashire County against Yorkshire. At the end of his second season he severed his connection with the Rovers, through failing to come to terms with the committee. While with Mellor and St. John's, Porter participated in many exciting ties in connection with the Rovers' medal competitions, for which he holds gold medals presented to the winners, as does his brother, Alec. Porter, an outside-right, who occasionally assisted the Rovers' Reserves, but is better known as a dashing member of the Mellor and St. John's forward lines. After leaving the Rovers, Walter Porter damaged his left knee while playing for Mellor against St. Francis', Feniscliffe, but subsequently was able to turn out for Thursday Rangers and St. Silas's.

The practice matches in August, 1896, produced quite a casualty list. Blackburn hurt himself by unexpectedly stepping on the ball with his left heel during a scrimmage in the goalmouth; Tierney twisted a knee, Jos. Hargreaves fractured a collar-bone, and Devlin, from Cambuslang, a reserve back, had his leg spiked so badly that he had to go off for the rest of the game, while early in September he was an in-patient at the Blackburn Infirmary, for injuries received at Liverpool, when Geary fell on the back's leg and damaged the muscles.

To such straits were the committee reduced for players that Herbert Fecitt displayed his affection for the old club by volunteering his services. In company with Murray, he turned out with the reserve side, and the chronicler of the period recorded that "both felt the effects of the exercise."

Up to the end of the second month the "Blue and Whites," after an uncertain start, played grandly. They surrendered two points to West Bromwich Albion at Blackburn, in the opening fixture, but the next seven matches yielded them five victories and two draws. These dramatic achievements, which seemed to indicate a bold bid for the championship, can thus be summarised:— Sept. 5th (h), v. Liverpool, 1–0; 12th (a), v. Bolton Wanderers, 0–0; 19th (h), v. Sheffield Wednesday, 4–0; 26th (a), v. Wolverhampton Wanderers, 1–1; Oct. 3rd (h), v. Burnley, 3–2; 10th (a), v. Preston

North End, 3–1; 17th (h), v. Bolton Wanderers, 1–0.

The contest with Liverpool, refereed by Mr. C. E. Sutcliffe, was remarkable for the fact that though the ball was driven into the net seven times, only one goal counted. Stuart, after nonplussing the visiting keeper, was ruled offside, and Chippendale will probably not yet have forgotten that just before the ball sailed under the bar from his characteristic shot the whistle sounded for the interval. In the second half the "Blue and Whites" thrice beat Storer, the Liverpool custodian, but on each occasion the points were negatived for offside. McVean then headed past Ogilvie, whose prompt appeal for offside was upheld. Late in the game, Stuart scored the solitary goal that was allowed, following a pretty movement in which Campbell and Chippendale participated. While Campbell and Wilkie, the home left-wing, were hailed as the "heroes of the fight," the team generally were applauded for a sterling exhibition. A sharp eye was kept on Jimmy Ross, one of the Preston "Invincibles," but now wearing the Liverpool colours. Though his shooting had not the power it formerly possessed, he required careful shadowing, and was allowed few liberties. In the second half Ross dislocated his shoulder. It was dressed on the field by a doctor, and the old North Ender pluckily played to the finish.

The Rovers' star was still in the ascendant when they entertained Sheffield Wednesday, who had defeated Wolverhampton Wanderers in the final of the F.A. Cup competition. Invested with all the prestige and glamour attaching to the Cup-holders, the Yorkshiremen were accorded a hearty Lancashire welcome, followed by a trouncing on the field. Though rain fell heavily, it affected neither the spirits nor the play of the "Blue and Whites," represented by Ogilvie; Brandon and Killean; Dewar, Anderson and Houlker; Wilmington (from Burnley), Chippendale, Tierney, Wilkie and Campbell. A crop of exciting incidents kept the crowd in a merry mood. There was a deep-throated cheer when Wilkie drove in a shot that almost shattered the cross-bar, but 35 minutes passed before Tierney opened the scoring. With this slender advantage against an admittedly smart side, who had combined cleverly and had often come to grips with the home defence, the Rovers had to contend with the wind and rain in the second half. This circumstance, however, did not reduce their dash or efficiency. After the visitors had repelled several hot attacks, the "Blue and Whites" scored twice in as many minutes, through Wilkie and Chippendale. These successes were in the nature of a knock-out blow to the Cup-holders, who went "all to pieces," with the exception of Spikesley and Brady, but their splendid example failed to animate their disheartened colleagues. So completely were the Rovers masters of the situation that they rested on their laurels, and then added a fourth goal for the delectation of their supporters.

One of those comical incidents that vastly amuse a football crowd occurred the following Saturday at Wolverhampton. After a rather longer interval than usual, the teams lined up to restart the game. A wag on the ground, noticing that the master of ceremonies was absent, piped a note. To his joy the "Wolves" burst off and were making tracks for the Rovers' goal when, arrested by the Homeric laughter of the spectators, they discovered the joke, but not the joker. At that moment Referee West dashed on to the field, and in response to ironical cheers doffed his cap to the chaffing crowd, who could not restrain their mirth. The visitors returned home with a point, for which they were principally indebted to Ogilvie, Brandon, and Killean, who played brilliantly.

Conscious of the fact that they had not "eaten the leek" in their last four games, the "Blue and Whites" were in fighting trim when Burnley came to Ewood with the avowed intention of capturing the spoils. An exceptionally large attendance testified to the keenness of the local rivalry, which was also manifested in the football. By a strange coincidence, neither of the regular custodians could appear. Joy, who deputised for Ogilvie, and Haddow, who was under the Burnley bar, probably never took part in a more exciting contest. Within 20 seconds the visitors scored without a Rover having touched the ball. This sensation was caused by the rapidity of Burnley's initial advance. On kicking-off, Robertson transferred to the left, where Bowes flashed past Brandon, and put the ball well across. Killean missed the centre, and while Joy was being bustled, Hill, the inside-right, rushed the ball into the net.

Stung to the quick by this sudden reverse, the Rovers showed that they could also move fast and furiously, but the cheers that rent the air as Tierney beat Haddow were turned into groans when offside was successfully claimed. Working splendidly together, the Burnley forwards severely taxed the Blackburn rearguard. During one of their determined assaults, Killean brought Hill to mother earth, with his feet uppermost. There was a yell of delight from the big contingent of Burnley spectators when a penalty was awarded. Joy, advancing to the six yards' mark, received Robertson's shot on his chest, and knocked the ball into safety. The enthusiasm aroused by this exploit gave place to derisive shouts when the referee ordered the penalty-kick to be retaken, because Brandon had stepped into the penalty area. Robertson made no mistake the second time, and Burnley crossed over leading 2–0.

That the home side had not lost courage, however, was evident by the briskness with which they commenced the second half. There were no laggards that afternoon. Every man was keyed to concert pitch. Early on, Dewar reduced the lead, and then the Rovers were granted a penalty from which Anderson equalised. This transformation upset the equanimity of the visitors, who were not as assertive as formerly, whereas the "Blue and Whites" were bubbling with mischief, and when Chippendale completed a thrilling run with a magnificent goal the Blackburn section of the crowd went into ecstasies. In the closing minutes the visitors rallied, and nearly drew level with a shot that rebounded from the foot of the post. It was one of those great matches that live in the memory and that redounded to the honour of the Rovers, whose dogged courage turned apparent defeat into glorious victory.

It is related of Dr. Morley that once when he met his brother, Viscount Morley of Blackburn, at the railway station, the distinguished statesman and litterateur proffered his handbag to the Doctor, who glared at him for a moment and then exclaimed,

"Carry your own bag! Do you think I am your blessed lackey?" If in this fiery manner he addressed his famous relative, for whom he had a deep affection, it requires no effort of the imagination to picture the heated scene that occurred on the Leamington-road ground when Dr. Morley came across W. A. McOwen in the Darwen club's colours. "Billy" McOwen was a first-class goalkeeper. He had served the Rovers faithfully and well for four seasons. In 1890 visions of an Association Cup medal, a priceless possession for any footballer, inspired him as he zealously performed his duties in all the matches that carried the "Blue and Whites" into the semi-final, from which they entered the final and won the coveted trophy for the fourth time by defeating Sheffield Wednesday 6–1. But just when his hopes were brightest McOwen was dropped!

J. K. Horne, of Accrington, who had an advantage in the matter of height, was selected for the semi-final, also appearing in the final. This disdainful treatment roused the ire of the deposed custodian, and he transferred his services to the Peaceful Valley club. Dr. Morley, though, was apparently unaware of McOwen's secession. By a curious coincidence the Rovers' next match after winning up was a friendly with Darwen. Naturally McOwen turned out for his new love. On the field he came face to face with the redoubtable Doctor, who did "carry on" when he saw the former Rover in a strange garb. "What are you doing in that jersey?" he peremptorily demanded. "We are going to beat you to-day, Doctor!" was the unexpected reply. "Fiddlesticks!" said the Doctor; "come with me at once into the tent, and we will talk matters over." "No," answered McOwen, "I am going to wear this jersey and we are going to show you what we can do!" The Doctor stormed, but failed to make any impression on Darwen's new goalkeeper.

At this point Mr. Mitchell, the Rovers' secretary, intervened. "I will go and tell your uncle," he said, evidently believing that this dire threat would result in the capitulation of the determined youth, who was 19 years of age. But "Billy" merely laughed; he was not afraid of his uncle, Mr. T. Hacking, who kept goal for Olympic.

Eventually the Rovers' representatives, finding that persuasion was useless, abandoned the contest. "Billy," accordingly, kept goal for Darwen, and the "Blue and Whites" were beaten 1–0, though they were represented by their full Cup team, including Horne. As the visitors seldom crossed the half-way line the game really resolved itself into a duel between McOwen and the Rovers. "Billy" convinced all and sundry that afternoon that he was a grand custodian. It was a feather in his cap that his side succeeded in defeating the famous Cup-holders, and Dr. Morley's feelings were considerably ruffled when an exuberant Darwen supporter, referring to McOwen's prowess, shouted at the top of his voice, "You fed him on cold pudding. He has had turkey and ducks and geese this week!"

"Billy" was a football prodigy. As a schoolboy of 15 he kept goal for the Rovers, whom he joined in 1886, and with whom he remained four years. Before then he was under the bar for the Olympic, of which his uncle was the regular custodian. McOwen had the distinction of being the youngest goalkeeper in the English League, started in 1888. For 14 years he was in the first flight. During that period he saw service with various clubs, and frequently covered himself with glory. In his early days goalkeepers were afforded no protection. They were fair "game" for opposing forwards. It was customary during attacks, especially when corners were taken, for opponents to floor the custodian if he was not quick enough to avoid their rushes. Many a time McOwen found himself on the ground, with three or four opponents on top of him. Hard knocks were given and accepted as a matter of course.

To show the stuff of which he was made it is only necessary to mention that for several weeks he played with a broken finger rather than give up his place in the Darwen side, then in the First Division, The injury to the little finger of his left hand was sustained when he was making a clearance in a match against Wolverhampton Wanderers. On another occasion he had his nose fractured through coming into contact with Jamieson, of Bootle, in an exciting contest at Barley Bank.

While with the Rovers, McOwen deputised for "Herby" Arthur in a remarkable game at Blackburn against West Bromwich Albion. At the time (October, 1887) he was a mere schoolboy. That memorable afternoon no fewer than 13 goals were scored— seven by the "Blue and Whites" and six by their opponents. It was a dingdong struggle right up to the last second, but the Rovers just managed to emerge victorious. Both sets of forwards were in such sparkling mood that neither custodian would readily forget his experience, because, though often beaten, they saved far more shots than those that passed them.

After rendering fine service to the Peaceful Valley eleven, McOwen joined the team of "All Macs," on the formation of the Liverpool club, in 1893, the Mersey side including nine "Macs," all Scots except "Billy," who is a native of Blackburn. The new organisation soon made their presence felt in sporting circles. They began by carrying off the Liverpool Cup and heading the Lancashire League in their first season. Then they were promoted to the Second Division of the Football League, and to the astonishment of their contemporaries walked off with the championship, earning 50 points out of a possible 56. As Birmingham were second with 42 points and Notts County third with 39, the superiority of the "All Macs" was unquestioned. What made the performance stand out in bold relief was that it was accomplished without Liverpool sustaining a single defeat. It was a wonderful achievement, largely due to a brilliant rearguard, consisting of McOwen, Andy Hannah (a Scots international), and Duncan McLean.

"Billy" missed but three matches that season, and had only 13 goals scored against him. On the conclusion of the campaign Liverpool were anxious that he should devote the whole of his time to football, instead of following his profession as a dentist. As he could not see his way to thus jeopardise his future prospects, he retired from the side, though the club were very desirous that he should accompany them into the First Division. Subsequently Mr. McOwen was reinstated as an amateur, after which he assisted Blackpool. While wearing the West Lancashire club's colours he distinguished himself in a Lancashire Cup tie against Everton at Goodison Park. Everton fielded their full League side. Blackpool were not in the same class as their First Division opponents, who incessantly bombarded the visitors' goal. But McOwen and his backs put up a grand fight, and when the backs were almost worn out by their exertions "Billy" still kept his charge intact. The crowd heartily cheered the plucky defenders, who repulsed all onslaughts until the last two minutes, when in a desperate finish Everton scored twice. One of the goals was due to a miskick by a back, and the losers claimed that the other one ought to have been disallowed for offside. So masterly was the Blackpool goalkeeper's exhibition that the "Athletic News" made it the subject of a headline, their report of the game appearing under the capitals "McOwen v. Everton." During his career "Billy" had to face 13 penalty kicks, and he saved 12 of them, a truly remarkable record. Strangely enough the one that beat him was taken by Jimmy Forrest in a Lancashire Cup tie between Blackburn Rovers and Liverpool.

Mr. McOwen, who now resides in Bolton-road, considers that Jack Southworth had not an equal as a centre-forward, either as a shot, in providing opportunities for his colleagues, or in opening out play. G.O. Smith (Old Caithusians), Johnny Goodall (Preston North End and Derby County), and Jack Devey (Aston Villa) he ranks as magnificent attackers, but in his opinion they were inferior to Southworth. During the time he was with Darwen he had leisure to study John Ralph Leach, the left-back, who was such a skilful player that Mr. McOwen is convinced that if Leach had been with the Rovers he would have been another Crompton. Joe Marsden, who afterwards migrated to Everton, was also an outstanding member of the Darwen rear division when "Billy" was associated with the club.

CHAPTER VI. — ON THE BRINK OF DISASTER.

Effect of Insignificant Trifles — Cup Duels with Chorley — False Prophets from Derby — An Unforgettable Period —The Dreaded Test Matches — Burnley's Brain Wave — Rovers Escape Their Doom.

THE history of the Rovers contains several illustrations of the fact that what appear to be insignificant trifles sometimes lead to unforeseen results. For example, when the "Blue and Whites" visited West Bromwich Albion in January, 1895, they found the frozen Stoney Lane ground as hard as the proverbial nails. Whereas the Albion were equipped for this contingency with boots barred and felted, which gave them a splendid grip and a sure footing, the Rovers turned out with the usual studs in their boots. As a consequence they skated about in all directions. On the other hand, the home side were not inconvenienced by the conditions, and won 2–0. After the match the hope was expressed that the Rovers' authorities would be prepared for any such emergency in the future, and not lose games for the sake of proper boots.

The following December, though, the players were hampered in a similar manner at Gigg Lane, in the first League contest between Bury and the "Blue and Whites." On this occasion the Rovers wore new boots with felted soles, which were an absolute failure. The men could not keep their feet. They slid all over the place. Bury, however, did not suffer in this respect. Their boots enabled them to move at a terrific pace. In these circumstances the Blackburn rearguard were often hard pressed, but they gave so courageous a display that only once were their colours lowered in the first half. Fog hung over the ground, and it became so dense that at the interval the game was abandoned. This piece of good fortune, however, availed little, because when the fixture was replayed Bury asserted their superiority to the tune of 2–0.

It was in October, 1896, that boots next exercised an important bearing on the issue of a League encounter. On the morning that the Rovers were due to travel to Liverpool the bags containing their outfits were deposited on the Blackburn railway station by the trainer, who was early on the scene. After piling them on the platform, he went to stretch his legs, thinking nobody would interfere with the club's belongings. In his absence the baggage caught the eye of a vigilant porter. He threw it aboard the next outward-bound train; then vanished, nor was his identity ever discovered. The fact that the bags were missing became known some time before the Liverpool train was scheduled to depart. The station staff were interrogated. They were blissfully ignorant of what had happened to the goods. Search was made in all the waiting-rooms, the parcels office was overhauled, and every likely and unlikely nook and corner was visited, all to no purpose. The baggage had vamosed. Amid the excitement that prevailed Dr. Morley by no means hid his light under a bushel. The well-nigh frantic trainer and the railway staff heard some very straight talking from the Rovers' vice-president. But it did not produce the all-important bags. They were having a joy ride on the Lancashire and Yorkshire system. Telegrams were sent in various directions. Still there was no trace of the errant luggage. The party were therefore compelled to proceed without it.

Two of the players made a practice of carrying their own sports wardrobe. On this occasion they hugged themselves with glee. On reaching the Mersey city the directors purchased nine pairs of football boots; pants and jerseys were borrowed from the Liverpool club. When the team appeared on the field they were scarcely recognisable. The cut of their pantaloons was displeasing to the eye. Their strange apparel gave them the aspect

SEASON 1899-1900.

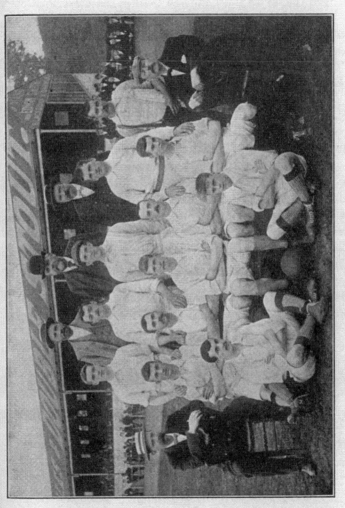

BACK ROW: J. CUNLIFFE, F. WOODHOUSE, T. GILLIBRAND (DIRECTORS).
MIDDLE ROW: R. HAWORTH, R. CROMPTON, THOMPSON, T. BRANDON, N. WALTON (TRAINER).
SITTING: J. WALMSLEY (SECRETARY), WILLIAMS, A. E. HOULKER, T. BOOTH, B. HULSE, D. HURST, M. HALLIWELL (DIRECTOR).
SITTING IN FRONT: T. BRIERCLIFFE, F. BLACKBURN.

of scarecrows rather than the usually spick and span Rovers. The new boots completed their discomfiture. Liverpool romped home 4–0. The Blackburn side's heavy reverse was attributed partly to their disarray, than which nothing is more calculated to depress a fastidious eleven.

Among the notable events of the disappointing campaign in 1896-7 was a clever victory over Bolton at Ewood Park when the so-called "small" team played astonishingly good football. The Wanderers, then at the height of their form, were the League leaders. They had won five of their seven matches, and divided the honours in the other two, one of which was against the "Blue and Whites" at Bolton. So powerful was the Wanderers' defence that it had yielded but four times prior to the visit to Blackburn, where they sustained their first defeat of the season by the narrow margin of a single goal. In a keen and exciting contest the Rovers established the lead in just under half an hour. Chippendale, in a tussle with Sutcliffe, the visiting custodian, secured possession of the ball, and slipped it to Tierney, who scored. Bolton vigorously appealed for off-side, but after consulting both linesmen, the referee found in favour of the Ewood representatives. In the last 10 minutes Nichol netted for Bolton. The point, though, was negatived by offside. That afternoon the Blackburn forwards, with Tierney as leader, were seen at their best. Had it not been for the brilliance of Sutcliffe, one of the finest custodians in the land and who was capped five times by England, the visitors would have met with a more emphatic reverse. It was on the following Saturday that the Rovers' baggage went gallivanting before the side entrained for Liverpool. That untoward occurrence, followed as it was by a severe defeat, marked the beginning of a decline, during which the "Blue and Whites" were pulverised at Derby (6–0) and were beaten 5–1 by Aston Villa at Ewood Park. The Rovers' attack at Derby was weakened by the loss of Tierney, who twisted a knee and had to be carried off. The centre-forward was often in the wars. He had any amount of pluck, and was always in the thick of scrimmages. In an earlier match, against Preston North End,

Tierney was kicked in the face. A few days later a sensation was caused by the widespread rumour that he had succumbed to the injury, but inquiry at his home at Chorley elicited the comforting information that the report was without the slightest foundation.

Towards the end of 1896 Nichol, of Burnley, was signed. In his first match against the Forest, at Nottingham, he partnered Brandon at full-back, but afterwards he operated usually as a forward.

"Geordie" Anderson, the Rovers' captain, was not only a magnificent half-back, but enjoyed a reputation as a sprinter. Following an easy victory in a foot race at Great Harwood, he was matched to run Charlie Athersmith, the Aston Villa forward, for £50 a side, over a distance of 110 yards, Anderson to receive three yards start. The fixture was arranged for January 8th, 1897, in the Midlands. However, a few days before it was due to take place the event was cancelled by order of the Rovers' committee. It was then announced that there were not likely to be any more races with Blackburn players as contestants.

The same month the Rovers and Chorley met for the third time in the first round of the Lancashire Cup, of which the "Blue and Whites" were the holders. As the two previous games had ended in draws, it was not surprising that great interest was manifested in the encounter at Burnden Park, Bolton, where the elevens were enthusiastically greeted by 5,000 spectators. The Blackburn men had prepared by taking breathers at Ribchester. Chorley had trained at Lytham. The Rovers' side consisted of Ogilvie; Brandon, Killean; Booth, Anderson, Houlker; Chippendale, Whitehead, Jos. Hargreaves, Wilkie, and Campbell. Their opponents relied on Pinnell; Ostick, Parker; Marton, McKennie, Thornborough; Waring, Mitchell, Cunliffe, Johnson, and Leadbetter.

The Blackburn supporters received a shock in a quarter of an hour, when Johnson scored for Chorley, whose defence, stimulated by this success, gave nothing away. The Rovers, though, were not to be denied. They were determined to win. While their attack had some difficulty in finding an opening, Anderson furnished them with a bright example by a surprise drive, which passed between Wilkie's legs before the ball came to rest in the net. This equaliser was obtained within eight minutes of the interval, and just before half-time the "Blue and Whites" gained the lead when a shot by Wilkie was deflected between the posts by Parker. It was expected that Chorley, with the wind in their favour, would be more dangerous in the concluding period. The pace, however, had been too hot for them. The Rovers were clearly the superior combination, and, going all out, gave the opposing rearguard no respite. Roughness developed, which somewhat spoilt the enjoyment of a hard contest. After Wilkie, an exceptionally clever performer, had had a goal disallowed for offside, Chippendale placed the result beyond doubt by a grand run three-parts the length of the ground, and with the co-operation of Hargreaves a third point was registered. This reverse so damped the spirits of Chorley that they lost heart. Thus, at the third time of asking, the Blackburn side revealed their old Cup-fighting qualities.

They did not, however, survive the next hurdle, for they came to grief at Ardwick, being beaten 1–0 by Manchester City. The defeat was a bitter blow for the "Blue and Whites," especially as City, in consequence of injuries, had five reserve players on view. While they were indisputably the better team, Blackburn could not get the ball past Williams, the Manchester custodian, who gave a marvellous display. He alone stood between the visitors and victory. It was a magnificent achievement on his part, but very disappointing to the County Cup holders, who for more than half the game were reduced to 10 men.

Shortly before the interval Campbell was kicked on the chin, and in falling was rendered unconscious by his head striking the frozen ground. As he lay prostrate, without the slightest movement, it was evident that his condition was serious. From all around the arena there were sympathetic cries of "Doctor !" The injured player was carried to the dressing room, where he was attended by two medical men. Later he was removed to a nursing home. A month elapsed before he was able to occupy his usual position. During the time that Campbell was laid aside, Sorley, an old Rover who had thrown in his lot with Hebburn Argyle, was also on the injured list with a broken nose, two black eyes and the loss of several teeth, which kept him out of the field for some weeks.

As the two Sheffield clubs had inflicted sensational defeats on the Ewood eleven, who were swamped 6–0 by the Wednesday and 7–0 by United, Derby County, with Johnny Goodall and Steve Bloomer among their forwards, fancied that the spoils were in their possession before the match started at Blackburn. So confident were they that on the railway journey they had informed fellow-travellers that they were certain to win 2–0. But they proved to be False prophets. While it is true they obtained two goals, they had not bargained for the fact that the Rovers would score five. The form shown that afternoon by Joy, Brandon, Killean, Dewar, Booth, Houlker, Nichol, Haylock, Hargreaves, Wilkie and Campbell sent the crowd into raptures. Killean particularly distinguished himself at left-back, and the forwards, admirably assisted by the halves, were a dashing quintet. Derby realised before the finish that it is never safe to prophesy about football. As some compensation for the League reverse, the "Blue and Whites" at Ewood Park knocked Sheffield United out of the Association Cup competition, in which the pair met for the first time. The Rovers triumphed by the odd goal in three. A sporting journal, commenting on the tie, paid a high tribute to Tom Booth, who was described as the best player on the field, and although this was his first season in the senior circle, "such well-known exponents as Dewar and Anderson, his confreres, are forced already to acknowledge his superiority." The Denton youth, who came to the Rovers from Ashton North End, quickly won his spurs, and was a valuable asset to the club.

During the late 'nineties the Rovers passed through a terrible period. Their descent towards Avernus mystified as well as disheartened their most loyal adherents. The splendour of their past was enveloped in a sable shroud. Tragedy stalked abroad. No glimmer of hope appeared on the horizon. So unfavourable were the portents that it seemed as if the famous old club could no longer remain in the glorious company of the elect. However long the "Blue and Whites" may grace the football arena, it is safe to predict that the agonising experience of 1898 will never be forgotten. For in that year the club tottered on the brink of disaster and nearly toppled into the yawning chasm of the Second Division. From that humiliation they were saved at the last moment by the extension of the League.

Many changes had been made in the side which had performed moderately the previous season. Such well-known figures as Ogilvie, Anderson, Dewar, Chippendale, Whitehead, Jos. Hargreaves, and Nichol disappeared. Ogilvie went to Shrewsbury Town, while Dewar, Anderson and Hargreaves transferred their services to New Brighton. To replace these men the directors did not tour Scotland for expensive recruits, but signed a number of more or less unknown players from the English shires, who were presented with a golden opportunity of making a reputation in first-class football. It had often been a reproach against the Rovers that they had not given adequate recognition to youths in Blackburn and district. Now, however, they placed on their pay sheet the pick of the men connected with local junior organisations, some of whom justified their selection for the reserve eleven.

For the seniors an understudy to Knowles was secured in J. Carter, a native of Preston, who had a good record as a custodian for Miliwall Athletic in the Southern League. Since Murray's retirement Killean and others had operated at left-back, but now Brandon was found a regular partner in J. Glover, of West Bromwich, who had performed meritoriously in the Midlands, where the usually astute Aston Villa committed an error of judgment in not snapping him up. The halves were strengthened by the inclusion of W. H. Ball, of Rock Ferry. While efforts were thus made to improve the rear divisions, attention was also paid to the attack. The Partick Thistle trio were the only forwards retained from the past season. They were supplemented by J. J. Bradbury, an outside-right of Ashton North End, Tom Booth's old club;

G. Hall, of Belfast Distillery, an Irish international and an inside-right who was something of a speed merchant; T. Briercliffe, of Blackburn, outside-right; and B. Hulse, of Rock Ferry, who could fill either of the inside-forward berths.

Obviously it was largely an experimental team. As the tournament progressed it became apparent that it was unequal to the exacting requirements of the First Division. Several other clubs were in a similar predicament. That, however, did not afford consolation to the "Blue and Whites," whose plight became more and more desperate. Their last three matches in the black Easter of 1898 were against Notts County, Bolton Wanderers and Bury. They required three points to escape the dreaded test games. To the chagrin of their followers, they did not succeed in obtaining them. Notts County prevailed 1–0 at Ewood Park, but hope was revived when Bolton, after a terrific struggle, were beaten 2–1 at Burnden Park. One point now spelt safety, but the Rovers had to meet Bury, who had been a thorn in their side ever since the Gigg-lane club had been promoted. As Bury were also fighting for their retention in the First Division, the excitement and anxiety in both camps needs no stressing. Every move of the encounter was eagerly watched by 10,000 spectators. In the result history repeated itself. By the only goal scored Bury won their salvation, while the Rovers, for the first time in their career, were in the Slough of Despond.

While such a situation was heart-rending, the crisis revealed that several old players had not lost their regard for the Blackburn club. Geordie Anderson, Jos. Hargreaves, Tommy Tierney, Harry Marshall (then with Heart of Midlothian), and Peter Turnbull (Glasgow Rangers) all rallied to its assistance and did their utmost to avert the calamity. Their chivalrous action showed that they were true sportsmen, and was highly appreciated in East Lancashire.

So rigorous had been the competition that that season Preston North End, Notts County, Bury, Blackburn Rovers and Stoke each finished with 24 points. Goal average, therefore, had to settle which two had to appear in the test matches. As the Rovers and Stoke were the worst off in this respect (the Rovers having scored 39 goals to 54 against, and Stoke 35 to 55), it was their fate to try conclusions with Burnley and Newcastle United, the leaders of the Second Division. Whereas the "Blue and Whites" had won but seven and lost 13 of their 30 engagements, Burnley in an equal number of matches had 20 victories against two defeats, and Newcastle had 21 successes to minimise their six reverses. Burnley had registered 80 goals against 24, and Newcastle 64 against 32.

In these crucial test games the Rovers sustained a double defeat by Burnley, losing 3–1 at Ewood and 2–0 at Turf Moor; and divided the points with Newcastle, winning 4–3 at Blackburn and being beaten 4–0 at St. James' Park. In the first contest with Burnley the "Blue and Whites" led 1–0 at the interval, but afterwards Toman did the "hat trick" for the visitors. In the return encounter Brandon and Booth, both injured, were unable to accompany their colleagues to Turf Moor. The weakened side, though, played stubbornly, but lacked sting forward. For the next of the series, against Newcastle, extreme measures were adopted. All the usual forwards were dropped except Hulse. Geordie Anderson was moved from centre-half to outside-right, as partner to Hulse; Jackson, of the reserve, replaced the injured Hargreaves as leader, and on his left he had Hurst and F. Blackburn. This bold policy succeeded. In a downpour of rain the scratch attack covered themselves with mud and glory. Four goals for the Rovers was a phenomenal achievement. Anderson was the hero of the match; he was the star member of the Blackburn vanguard. All the home goals were the outcome of his brilliance. Three of them accrued from his centres—Blackburn converting the first and Hurst the other two—while "Geordie" had the intense satisfaction of scoring the fourth with a splendid shot that Watts, the old Rover, who was under the bar for United, partly stopped, after which the ball rolled over his shoulder into the net.

With the score 4–2 in favour of the "Blue and Whites," Killean sustained a severe injury in effecting a clearance. It was believed he had broken his right leg. He was carried off on a board. Fortunately, the accident was not as serious as at first supposed, the

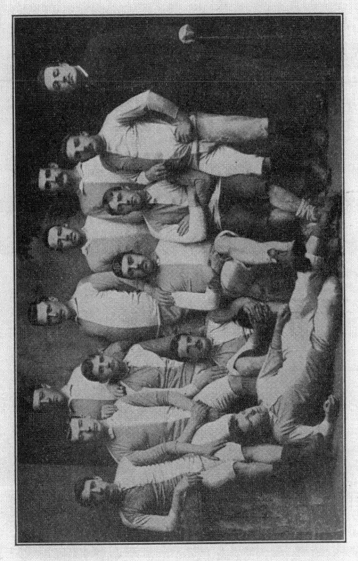

FAMOUS OLD ROVERS.

BACK ROW: D. GREENWOOD, ROGER HOWORTH, J. HARGREAVES, F. SUTER, W. DUCKWORTH (IN CIVILIAN ATTIRE).
SECOND ROW: J. DUCKWORTH, H. MCINTYRE, H. SHARPLES, F. HARGREAVES, T. STRACHAN, G. AVERY.
FRONT ROW: J. BROWN, WITH J. DOUGLAS NEXT TO HIM.

limb being badly bruised but no bones fractured. Reduced to 10 men in the last quarter of an hour against a powerful combination, the Rovers nevertheless clung to their advantage, and though their opponents scored a third goal, the Ewood representatives gained a remarkable victory. The final struggle at St. James' Park was marred by a regrettable occurrence. During a bombardment of the Blackburn goal the crowd on the popular side of the ground surged forward, causing a portion of the railings to suddenly collapse and throwing scores of people into a heap. A youth had a foot literally torn off, a boy broke his leg, and other spectators were treated for minor injuries.

As they had failed to survive the ordeal of the tests, the Rovers' doom appeared to be sealed. At this juncture, though, Burnley had a brain wave. They drafted a notice of motion that each division of the League should be increased from 16 to 18 clubs, that the test matches should be abolished, and that in future there should be automatic relegation and promotion, the two top clubs in the Second Division exchanging places with the two bottom clubs in the First Division. This proposal, which was cordially welcomed by the clubs in general, was carried at the annual meeting of the League. The news was received with unfeigned joy in Blackburn. It is an interesting fact that the previous season the Rovers had voted for an extension of the League, hence there was nothing inconsistent in their action in circularising the clubs to support the Burnley scheme. Nor should it be forgotten that while the issue hung in the balance the Blackburn club received a letter from Mr. G. B. Ramsay, on behalf of Aston Villa F.C., who, after mentioning that the Birmingham club would vote for the extension of the League, said, "If it is carried you will come back to the First Division, but if it is not, no one will regret it more than the club I have the honour to represent, and we will be pleased, for bare expenses, to come to Blackburn and play a benefit match in order to help you. Again I assure you of our sincere sympathy." All honour to the Villa for their sportsmanlike offer! So esteemed were the Rovers, even in the days of their misfortune, that genuine sorrow would have been felt all over the country if they had temporarily lost their status. From that affliction they were spared by the inspiration of Burnley and the benevolence of their confreres.

Early in the season Dr. Morley was paid a pretty compliment by Everton F.C., who invited him to open a magnificent new grandstand erected at Goodison Park. The Rovers' chairman, who was presented with a gold key with which to unlock the door, performed the ceremony in characteristic fashion, delivering a breezy speech, in which he replied to critics who asserted that the country was going mad on sport, especially football. He said he was one of those who believed in the greatest good of the greatest number. Football, he added, gave unalloyed pleasure to thousands of people every week, and he was convinced that the heart of England rejoiced at the success of the great winter pastime.

CHAPTER VII. — BRILLIANT CUP-FIGHTERS.

Superb Exploits — Six Times in F.A. Cup Final — Three Consecutive Triumphs — Record Scoring in Classic Encounter — Blackburn Player's Distinction — Old Etonians Spring a Surprise — Kinnaird's Gymnastic Feat.

THE Rovers achieved national distinction by their brilliance as cup fighters. They were the first provincial team to challenge the supremacy of the south in the final of the Association Cup competition. For 10 years the trophy had been won by clubs in the Metropolitan area and Oxford University, but after 1881-2, when the Rovers made their initial bid for fame, the old order changed. At the second attempt Blackburn, through the medium of the Olympic, administered the *coup de grace* to the southern stalwarts.

The "Blue and Whites," who have appeared six times in the classic encounter, have had the honour of winning the Cup on five occasions. For three seasons in succession they carried off the coveted trophy, a superb exploit, though not a record, as the feat had been performed previously by the London Wanderers, who, when the Cup became their absolute property in 1878, handed it back to the Association on condition that it was not to be won outright by any club. On account of this stipulation the Rovers were presented with a handsome silver shield in commemoration of their third consecutive triumph in 1886. It now adorns the Board Room at Ewood Park. Apart from the Wanderers and the "Blue and Whites," no club has succeeded in capturing the Cup thrice in succession. The Rovers were the first side to score six goals in a final, when they defeated Sheffield Wednesday 6–1 in 1890. This remained a record until Bury beat Derby County 6–0 in 1903. In the 50 finals that have been played so far, these two Lancashire teams are the only ones with half-a-dozen goals to their credit. Another historical fact is that the Rovers took part in the first final staged in the provinces, the replay against West Bromwich Albion at Derby in 1886, when the Midland representatives were vanquished 2–0. Mr. James Forrest, now a director of the Rovers' F.C., is the proud possessor of five Association Cup medals, a distinction shared with Mr. C. H. R. Wollaston (The Wanderers) and Lord Kinnaird (The Wanderers and Old Etonians), both of whom have passed to that bourne whence no traveller returns. W. Townley's magnificent achievement in scoring three goals in a final, in 1890, stands unequalled, while "Herby" Arthur was on the winning side in three Association Cup finals, an honour held by no other custodian.

Aston Villa occupy pride of place as Cup finalists, with six victories in eight appearances. The London Wanderers won all their five finals. The Old Etonians, West Bromwich Albion and Newcastle United have figured six times in the great event, and have each been successful twice. In five finals Wolverhampton Wanderers were twice victorious. Preston North End and Bolton Wanderers have won the trophy once, though they have been in three finals; Bury were successful on the two occasions they earned the right to be in the last round, scoring 4–0 against Southampton in 1900 and 6–0 against Derby County in 1903. With R. Sewell (now of the Rovers) under the bar, Burnley in the only appearance they have made in the final beat Liverpool 1–0 in 1914.

When the Rovers, as the hope of the North, left for London in March, 1882, they were regarded as almost invincible. They had had a wonderful season, unchequered by a single reverse. Of their 35 matches they had won 31 and drawn four, and had scored no fewer than 192 goals against 33. In the earlier stages of the Cup competition they had registered 28 goals against 6. Park Road were their victims by 9–1, Bolton Wanderers were vanquished

6–2, and after a bye in the third round, they defeated Darwen, then their equals, by 5–1. An away victory of 3–1 over Wednesbury Old Athletic, a strong Midland organisation, paved the way to the semi-final, with sterling Sheffield Wednesday as their opponents.

In the tie with Park Road on the Leamington-road ground, in October, 1881, the Rovers were represented by R. Howorth, goal; D. H. Greenwood and F. Suter, backs; H. McIntyre and F. W. Hargreaves (capt.), half-backs; J. Duckworth and J. Douglas (right wing), J. Brown and T. Strachan (centre-forward), and G. Avery and J. Hargreaves (left wing). The Park Road team was composed of W. Wilson, goal; J. W. Pickup and J. Jefferson, backs; T. McQuirk and J. Walmsley, half-backs; J. Hartley and A. Mackereth (right wing), J. McQuirk and J. Pemberton (centre-forward), and J. Nuttall and W. Whalley (left wing). Avery was responsible for four of the nine goals obtained by the "Blue and Whites"; Brown, Douglas and Strachan were credited with one each, another accrued from a corner taken by Brown, and the last followed a shot by F. Hargreaves, the ball after striking the bar glancing off a defender between the posts. Nuttall was the successful Park Road marksman. Against Bolton the goal scorers were Avery, Brown (2), McIntyre (2) and Sharples.

Though they had surmounted the previous obstacles with comparative ease, a stern struggle awaited the Rovers when they faced Sheffield Wednesday in the semi-final, on the St. John's ground, Huddersfield, with the object apparently of popularising Association football in a Rugby stronghold. The extraordinary action of sprinkling cinders on the turf, after rain, was a positive menace to the players, some of whom sustained nasty cuts in a very vigorous contest. Brown and Duckworth, the Blackburn light-weights, came in for severe treatment, the dapper little centre-forward having an opponent told off to pay him unremitting attention. When the secret leaked out before the elevens emerged from the dressing-tent, Brown nonchalantly remarked that he had been knocked down before and had survived, All the same, he was black and blue with bruises before the end of the 90 minutes, and was once robbed of an almost certain goal by a back charge that sent him sprawling among the cinders. Whereas the Rovers played two halves and six forwards, their opponents adopted the newer style of three halves and five forwards, and occasionally packed their goal with seven defenders. Sheffield had dismissed the Rovers from the Cup competition the previous season, hence the keenness of the rivalry. The Lancastrians were anxious to avenge that defeat, and the Yorkshiremen were equally determined to appear in the final. In the second half Avery drove the ball between the posts, but the point was disallowed for hands. As neither custodian had his colours lowered the sides lived to fight another day. Special significance attached to the result, because it was the first match in which the Rovers had failed to score that season. It was suggested that their inability to reproduce their customary form arose from the fact that the saloon in which the players travelled to Huddersfield was packed with enthusiasts, was thick with tobacco smoke, and that the conversation so excited the players as to make them less fit for their duties on the field. Be that as it may, it is certainly true that in the concluding period "every man worked harder for honour than ever he would for pay," also that with ordinary luck the team might have scored two or three times. The Blackburn men were anxious to continue for an extra half-hour, but after consultation between the captains, umpires and referee, the proceedings were adjourned.

Sheffield had the same team in the replay at Whalley Range, Manchester, but the "Blue and Whites" were deprived of the services of D. H. Greenwood who had been injured in an international match. McIntyre filled the vacancy at full back, and H. Sharples, of the second eleven, was drafted into the half-back line. On this occasion the Rovers atoned for any shortcomings they had shown at Huddersfleld by winning brilliantly by 5–1. Ten thousand spectators, including a large contingent from Blackburn, had an early thrill when a dashing raid by Avery, Douglas and Duckworth developed into a fierce scrimmage in the Wednesday goalmouth. The custodian went to earth to stop the ball; in a few seconds half-a-dozen men were on top of him, all struggling as if for dear life. The attackers pushed the goalkeeper and the ball between the posts, but as neither of the umpires saw the accomplishment of this feat no goal was allowed. Ultimately the ball came out a short distance and Duckworth then screwed it wide. At the end of 20 minutes the Rovers received a setback when their captain, in attempting to head away from Malpas, put the ball through his own goal. However, eight minutes before the interval, J. Hargreaves equalised, after clever work by his brother and McIntyre. So far Sheffield had had the wind at their backs and had played down the slope, while the Rovers had had the sun in their eyes. Now it was Blackburn's turn to benefit by the conditions, and they quickly proved themselves masters of the situation. Through Avery and Douglas they added two goals in 14 minutes, and in the last two minutes put on another couple, the fourth point following a fine throw-in by F. Hargreaves, which enabled Douglas to deliver an accurate shot that went through off a defender, and the last one was obtained by Suter from a corner splendidly placed by Brown. The Rovers' captain particularly excelled, and Sharples fully justified his selection.

The victors were enthusiastically greeted on arriving at Blackburn. As the train steamed into the station fog signals were exploded on the line. Later various members of the team were carried shoulder high through the principal streets. It was a regular gala night.

The other finalists were the celebrated Old Etonians, captained by Lord Kinnaird (then the, Hon. A. F.), who was noted for his tenacity and vigour. In sporting circles the momentous game formed practically the sole subject of conversation. On the eve of the match, which took place at Kennington Oval on March 25th, 1882, the "Sportsman" announced that the Rovers were favourites, odds of six to four being laid on them in the city. The wiseacres, though, were out of their reckoning, because the Old Etonians won the Cup, for the second and last time in their career, by a goal scored by Anderson eight minutes from the start.

Kinnaird, a half-back, who turned out in long white trousers and wore a beard, which made him doubly conspicuous, was so elated by Anderson's success that he celebrated the event by standing on his head in front of the pavilion, providing possibly the only instance in which the scion of a noble house has given such a gymnastic display on a football field. He was cheered to the echo by Etonians, enraptured by the display of the Old Boys.

Among the 6,000 spectators were a thousand from East Lancashire. The teams were :—Old Etonians: J. F. P. Rawlinson goal; T. H. French and P. J. de Paravicini, backs; Hon. A. F. Kinnaird (capt.) and C. W. Foley, half-backs; W. J. Anderson and J. B. T. Chevallier (right wing), R. H. Macaulay and H. C. Goodart (centre-forwards), P. C. Novelli and A. T. B. Dunn (left wing). Blackburn Rovers: R. Howorth, goal; H. McIntyre and F. Suter, backs; H. Sharples and F. W. Hargreaves (capt.), half-backs; J. Duckworth and J. Douglas (right wing), T. Strachan and J. Brown (centre-forwards), G. Avery and J. Hargreaves (left wing).

Three factors militated against the East Lancashire visitors. On the morning that the Rovers left for London a letter arrived from Mr. C. W. Alcock, then secretary of the Football Association, intimating that it would be necessdry for them to change their colours, as they were similar to those of their opponents. They donned black and white shirts, which gave them an unfamiliar aspect. Even now it is asserted that the changing of the colours lost them the match. In the second place, their rivals won the toss, carrying with it the advantage of a strong wind, which in the concluding half almost disappeared. The third, and most important, circumstance was that the Lancastrians were obliged to combat a style of play with which they were unacquainted. Indulging in none of the dribbling and dodging which were attractive features of the Rovers' display, the Old Etonians relied on rushes, supplemented by weight, speed, and fancy kicking. While dashing along they frequently sprang into the air to kick the ball, with both feet off the ground. Whether opponents were near at hand made no difference. Strangers to this peculiar practice, the Blackburn men were often badly hurt, particularly in the closing stages, when they penned their antagonists in their own quarters. With the visitors constantly striving to equalise the last 20 minutes witnessed a desperate struggle, in which the Southerners just managed to retain their grip on the game. Suter, who gave a magnificent exhibition, Strachan, Duckworth and Mcintyre added to their laurels. Their colleagues also played skilfully, but on the whole the team did not reach their most brilliant form. For the winners Kinnaird and Foley stood out prominently, and Rawlinson far exceeded expectations.

Those present at this historic encounter included Mr. W. E. Briggs and Sir Wm. Coddington, the Parliamentary representatives for Blackburn, who after the match entertained the Rovers and a few friends to dinner; Major Gen. Feilden, C.M.G., of Witton Park, lord of the manor and junior member for the northern division of the County Palatine; Mr. John Lewis, founder of the club; Mr. Richard Birtwistle, one of the original playing members and a great forward in his day, and Dr. Morley. When the team reached Blackburn on the following Tuesday evening they were welcomed by a brass band, two pipers, and thousands of the inhabitants, who accorded them a tremendous reception in recognition of their splendid efforts to capture the national trophy for Lancashire.

F.A. Cup Winners, 1884.

Back Row : J. Lofthouse, H. McIntyre, J. Beverley, H. Arthur, F. Suter, J. H. Forrest, R. Birtwistle (Umpire).
Front Row : J. Douglas, J. Sowerbutts, J. Brown, G. Avery, J. Hargreaves.
Trophies : East Lancashire Charity Cup, Football Association Cup, L.F.A. Cup.

CHAPTER VIII. — THREE SUCCESSIVE CUP VICTORIES.

Bringing Home the Cup — Pride of Lancashire v. Flower of Scotland — The "Northern Horde" — Rovers' second Victory Over Queen's Park — Boat Race Sequel — Brown's Wonderful Dribble — Fecitt's Brilliance Against the Albion.

W HEN the all-conquering Rovers brought the Association Cup home in March, 1884, the enthusiasm of the inhabitants knew no bounds. The square in front of the railway station was packed with a cheering multitude, and the main streets were almost impassable owing to the dense throngs who had assembled to welcome the heroes of the occasion. An imposing procession, containing seven large equipages, was led by the Borough Brass Band, behind whom rode the victorious team, in a gaily beflagged wagonette, drawn by six spanking greys. Next came the committee and members of the Press, who were followed by representatives of the Olympic (late holders of the trophy), in a big conveyance, decorated with flags and drawn by eight horses, with three postillions in red jackets and velvet caps. Behind them rode members of the Park Road club, and in another carriage Mr. John Brown, father of the Rovers' captain, was a prominent figure. The Livesey Brass Band, in uniform, brought up the rear.

In celebration of the event flags and streamers adorned the principal thoroughfares, where many buildings were beautifully embellished. In Penny Street a grand display was given by Mr. John Boyle, tailor, from whose artistically decorated shop front

103

depended balloons and streamers. Illumination was supplied by
electric arc lamps, for which special plant was installed. When the
procession drew up in front of the shop, with Jimmy Brown waving
the Cup aloft, scores of coloured lights flashed and sparkled. A
well-known Blackburn tradesman, then a lad, is still proud of the
fact that he was one of those selected by Mr. Boyle to act as a
"shovel boy" in connection with the pyrotechnic display on that
never-to-be-forgotten night.

On their second visit to the Oval the "Blue and Whites"
did not suffer from that over-confidence to which some shrewd
judges attributed their defeat by the Old Etonians. This time their
opponents were Queen's Park, the flower of Scotland, who were
the first club from over the Border to take part in the national
competition, in which their debut was so sensational that now
they had the distinction of pitting their skill in the concluding
stage against the most popular club in England. On three previous
occasions the Rovers and Queen's Park had met in other events,
without either being able to obtain a victory. The Cup final,
therefore, resolved itself into an international contest so unique
as to be without precedent and so important as to have no parallel
in the annals of Association football. If the Rovers needed any
incentive to live up to their reputation it was furnished by the
knowledge that their rivals had defeated Blackburn Olympic
(holders of the trophy) in the semi-final, whereas if the Olympic
had won that match another wonderful record would have been
established by two clubs from the same town appearing in the
final.

A strange incident happened in the Rovers' semi-final against
Notts County, at Birmingham. Their antagonists were so rough
that they were often hooted by the crowd for heavy charging. As
soon as play ceased the Notts men ran to the umpire and left the
field under his protection, from which it was apparent that they
knew they had incurred the severe displeasure of the spectators. In
this hard struggle the "Blue and Whites" prevailed 1–0, the goal
being scored in the second half by Lofthouse, after whose success

Avery, Strachan and Douglas fell back to strengthen the rearguard. This manoeuvre was so effective that for the second time in an important contest Arthur, in goal, never handled the ball and had only once to kick it in defence of his charge. The County lodged an unsuccessful protest against Jock Inglis on the ground that he was an imported professional.

With 13 tried and trusted players available, the committee had a thankless task in choosing the side to do duty in the great contest at the Oval on March 29th. When it was rumoured that Jack Hargreaves was to be omitted there was such indignation among the supporters of the club that a special meeting of the committee was convened to consider the matter. As a result Hargreaves was included to the exclusion of Avery, who had played in the 1882 final. In fact there were six changes in the personnel of the eleven as compared with that against the Old Etonians. Those who took part in both finals were Fergie Suter, a popular idol, formerly of Partick and Darwen, and who was one of the giants of the Blackburn eleven; Hugh McIntyre, who before coming to the "Blue and Whites" saw service with Partick and Glasgow Rangers, and was a gifted exponent as a back, a half-back, or a forward; Jimmy Douglas, formerly of Renfrew, who, when the odds were against the Rovers became impervious to danger and was a terror in scrimmages; Jimmy Brown, who learned his football at Mintholme College, as a mere mite joined the club in 1879, at the early age of 17, was one of the youngest players to don an international jersey (in the season 1880-81), and was a brilliant leader of the attack; and Jack Hargreaves, also an international, who never tired, was a dangerous shot, and was one of the best left wingers in the country.

Over 10,000 spectators gave the opposing forces a hearty welcome as they lined up as under :— Blackburn Rovers: H. Arthur, goal; J. Beverley and F. Suter, backs; Forrest and H. McIntyre, half-backs; J. Lofthouse and Douglas (right wing), J. Brown (captain), and J. Inglis (centre forwards), J. Sowerbutts and J. Hargreaves (left wing). Queen's Park: G. Gillespie;

W. Arnott and J. MacDonald; C. Campbell (capt.) and J. J. Gow; W. Anderson, W. W. Watt, Dr. Smith, W. Harrower, D. S. Allan, and R. M. Christie.

In a very fast game the Scots quickly showed that they meant business. Early on Christie beat Arthur, but was ruled offside. Then Arnott from a free kick struck the bar, the ball dropping between the posts. However, as the ball had not touched a second player the goal did not count. The Rovers, though, did their share of pressing, and opened their account at the end of half-an-hour. An advance in which Sowerbutts and Hargreaves co-operated resulted in Brown scoring after skilfully eluding Arnott and Gillespie. Forrest had the satisfaction of registering a second goal. Four minutes from the interval Christie outwitted the Rovers' custodian with a high shot. In the second half Gillespie dropped a fast drive from Brown, scooping the ball out. It was claimed it had passed between the posts. The appeal, though, was disallowed. Later Douglas headed through, only to be given offside. Thus the Rovers conquered the pride of Scotland by 2–1. Arthur, making his first appearance in the final, surpassed all his displays as a custodian, and the side as a whole performed magnificently, Jock Inglis cried for joy after the match. He kept repeating, "I'm the only Scot to take a medal home!"

The "Sportsman" in its comments said: "Forrest, at half-back, cannot be too highly commended whilst forward special mention may be made of Lofthouse, Brown and Sowerbutts, the last-named showing wonderful form for a youth." "Sporting Life" observed that "the combination of the winners' forwards was as good as the defence of their backs was excellent. Beverley and Forrest, in particular, deserve the highest praise for their accurate kicking and tackling. The English backs showed generally to advantage in comparison with those of Scotland. The Rovers thoroughly deserved their victory."

Owing to the death of the Duke of Albany, the Cup and medals were not publicly presented at the Oval. They were quietly handed to Brown by Major Marindin, president of the Football

Association, who had refereed the game. During the match scores of pigeons were released by Lancashire visitors, who were described by a London newspaper as the "Northern horde," an epithet that was deeply resented. The borough members, Mr. Briggs and Sir William Coddington, again entertained the players and committee to dinner. It was a joyous feast. Mr. Briggs, alluding to the time when football used to be played in the Strand, said an eminent divine then declared the game to be "a bloody and murthering practice rather than a fellowly sport or pastime." He disagreed entirely with the rev. gentleman, because football was a sport demanded skill, endurance, and a great amount of training.

With one or two exceptions the Rovers were able to rely on the same team and as each member possessed exceptional skill they were a formidable combination, yielding pride of place to none. They retained possession of trophy in 1884-5 by handsomely defeating seven clubs, viz.: Rossendale, 11–0; Blackburn Olympic, 3–2; Witton, 5–1; Romford, 8–0; West Bromwich Albion, 2–0; Old Carthusians (semi-final), 5–1; and Queen's Park, Glasgow (final), 2–0.

The heavily built Romford team, who were expected to extend the Cup holders, cut a sorry figure in the tie at Blackburn. Some misgiving, however, was entertained with regard to the visit to West Bromwich, as the Rovers had hoped to strengthen their forces by the inclusion of Geo. Haworth, of Accrington, and Tot Rostron, who went from Darwen to Great Lever, but were prevented uncharitable decree of the Football Association. The edict, however, failed of its purpose. It roused the fighting spirit of the "Blue and Whites," and the Albion had to pay the penalty. In the semi-final against the Old Carthusians, at Nottingham, it was thought that the Lancastrians would "just win," as the attack had to meet a celebrated pair of backs in the brothers A. M. and P. M. Walters. To the general surprise the Old Boys' defence was riddled by the active Blackburn forwards.

A piquant situation was created when Queen's Park, who had also been performing valorous deeds, again qualified for the final.

Sporting circles were greatly excited at the prospect of a renewal of the combat between last year's rivals in the classic encounter. This Homeric contest took place at the Oval on April 4th, 1885. The Rovers had altered their field formation to three halves and five forwards, but their opponents retained the old style of two halves and six forwards. Jack Hargreaves, Beverley and Inglis were absentees on this occasion, the vacancies being filled by Herbert Fecitt, R. G. Turner and Geo. Haworth. Queen's Park had likewise some changes.

The game attracted the largest crowd that had assembled at a football match in London, estimated at from 12,000 to 18,000. The teams were :—Blackburn Rovers: H. Arthur, goal; R. G. Turner and F. Suter, backs; G. Haworth, H. McIntyre and J. Forrest half-backs; J. M. Lofthouse, J. Douglas, J. Brown (capt.), H. Fecitt, J. Sowerbutts, forwards. Queen's Park: G. Gillespie; W. Arnott and W. MacLeod; C. Campbell (capt.) and J. MacDonald; A. Hamilton, W. Anderson, W. Sellar, W. Gray, N. McWhannel, and D. S. Allan.

To the consternation of their compatriots, the Scots were decisively beaten. Campbell and his gallant band had shown such consistent form that season that they stepped on to the field confident of their ability to vanquish their Lancashire foes. But Blackburn pluck and Blackburn skill triumphed gloriously. Queen's Park had a demon dodger in Anderson, but he was put in the shade by the dashing Brown, who played as if inspired. Barely 14 minutes had elapsed when the Rovers' captain crashed the ball with such force against the crossbar that the stout timber quivered. The ball rebounded over the heads of the backs, and, quick as lightning, Forrest drove it between the posts. The half-back thus had the distinction of scoring in each of the two finals in which he had appeared, for the previous season he registered the Rovers' winning goal against the same club. In the second half Brown relieved pressure by a characteristic dash. In midfield MacLeod fell on him, but the check was only momentary, as Fecitt, gathering the ball, rounded Hamilton, McWhannel and Sellar. Then he placed the ball forward, slightly to his right, presenting Brown, who had followed up, with an easy chance, and the Rovers' captain had no difficulty in adding a second goal 20 minutes from the end. Instead of avenging their previous reverse, Queen's were well and truly beaten by the "Blue and Whites," whose forwards gave a magnificent exhibition, Brown, Sowerbutts and Fecitt especially excelling. In a strong half-back line Haworth was awarded the palm, with Forrest nearly his equal. The ultimate defence had less work to do than they expected. Indeed, Arthur only thrice handled the ball, on each occasion in the second half. Brown and Lofthouse were carried shoulder high off the field. Major Marindin publicly presented the Cup and medals to the victors, who were enthusiastically cheered.

By disposing of Clitheroe, 2–0; Oswaldtwistle Rovers, 1–0; Darwen Old Wanderers, 6–1; Staveley (previously undefeated that season), 7–1; Brentwood, 3–1; and London Swifts (semi-final), 2–1; the "Blue and Whites" had the rare distinction of making a third successive appearance at the Oval, where they effected a goalless draw with West Bromwich Albion, on April 3rd, 1886. The Staffordshire side consisted of R. Roberts; H. Green and H. Bell; E. Horton, C. Perry and Timmins; G. Woodhall, T. Green, J. M. Bayliss, A. Loach, and G. Bell. There were two changes in the Blackburn team compared with 1885—J. Heyes for Haworth at right half, and Strachan for Lofthouse at outside right.

That the doughty Lancashire cup-fighters did not force a definite issue is capable of a simple explanation. Before the match they were thoroughly chilled through watching the Boat Race, they scamped their lunch, and left themselves barely time to drive to Kennington and strip for the final. In the closing minutes Fecitt made a great effort to secure victory. Nearly everybody thought he had scored, but his shot hit one of the ropes and glanced behind on the wrong side of the post. Suter and Turner, notwithstanding that the latter sprained his ankle, played superbly, and Arthur gave a thrilling exhibition in goal. These three were the undoubted saviours of the side.

When the teams met a week later, at Derby, Douglas was at half-back in place of Heyes, and Walton partnered Strachan on the right wing. The Albion were as before. As a result of a raid in which Walton and Fecitt were prominent, Sowerbutts scored after 26 minutes. The same player again beat Roberts, but no appeal was made for a goal, as the forward was in an offside position, though it afterwards transpired that the referee (Major Marindin) would have allowed the goal, if there had been a claim, seeing that the ball had touched an opponent before it reached Sowerbutts. At half-time the Rovers led 1–0. With 17 minutes to play Brown sent the crowd into ecstasies by one of the most spectacular performances seen on a football field. At the time the Albion were striving hard for an equaliser, but McIntyre returned the ball, and Brown, eluding Green in midfield, dribbled rapidly along right wing, with Green in hot pursuit. Curving as he neared goal, he paused an instant to take aim, and just as Green was upon him, sent the ball skimming through the further corner of the goal, out of the reach of the custodian. Arthur again distinguished himself. During the presentation of the Cup and medals he was specially complimented by Major Marindin, who declared that the Rovers' triumph, by 2–0, was due in great measure to the skill of the Blackburn goalkeeper. By common consent Fecitt, who was irresistible, was the best forward on the field; he was simply brilliant. Forrest was an outstanding member of a powerful defence. By these superb achievements the "Blue and Whites" inscribed their names on the everlasting Scroll of Fame.

F.A. Cup Winners, 1890.

Back Row: James Southworth, John Southworth, R. Birtwistle, J. K. Horne, G. Dewar.
Middle Row: J. M. Lofthouse, H. Campbell, J. Forbes (Captain), N. Walton, W. Townley.
Front Row: J. Barton, J. H. Forrest.

CHAPTER IX. — CUP FINALS IN THE 'NINETIES.

Heavy Scoring at the Oval — Sheffield Wednesday's Stage Fright — Townley's Record Achievement — Notts County's Sensational Rehearsal of the Cup Final — What Happened a Week Later — Lancashire Cup Finals.

AFTER the lapse of four years the "Blue and Whites" again had the honour of participating in the Association Cup final, March 29th, 1890. There were many new faces in the side. Of the players who had reached the pinnacle of fame in the eighties but three remained— Forrest, Lofthouse and Walton. Under Forbes' captaincy the team had attained such efficiency that it was regarded as "undoubtedly better than the combination which last appeared at the Oval on behalf of the club in 1886." With the exception of J. K. Horne and James Southworth, all the Rovers were internationals. Their ranks included no fewer than six natives of Blackburn in the brothers James and John Southworth, John Barton, James H. Forrest, Joseph Lofthouse and Wm, Townley; two other Lancastrians in Horne, of Accrington, and Nat. Walton, of Preston, and three Scots in John Forbes, Geordie Dewar and Harry Campbell.

Sheffield Wednesday, their opponents, were making their first appearance in the classic encounter. They rejoiced in the fact that not only were all their players English, but, with one exception, local products. Among the clubs they overcame in the preliminary rounds were Accrington (2–1) and Bolton Wanderers (semi-final) by the same score.

On the other hand, the Rovers almost stumbled on the threshold, as extra time was necessary to enable them to vanquish Sunderland by 4–2 in the first round at Blackburn; but in the succeeding ties, up to the final, their defence was invulnerable. Grimsby Town were beaten 3–0, Bootle 7–0, and Wolverhampton Wanderers (semi-final) 1–0, giving a total of 15 goals to 2.

The doors of the Oval were thrown open at one o'clock, and by 3-30 the attendance exceeded 20,000. The scarlet jackets of the military, allowed free access, relieved the dark monotony of the ring. Later, when the crowd became unmanageable, the soldiers helped a strong body of police to keep order. On this account it was expected that the next time some of the London newspapers, whose allusions to the "Northern horde" had not been forgotten or forgiven, entertained their readers with football fables they would dwell on "the military having to be called out to preserve order." A roar of applause greeted the Rovers, who were in white jerseys and white knickers, but a still greater burst of cheering heralded the appearance of the Wednesday, who were attired in blue jerseys. The teams were :—Blackburn Rovers: Horne; James Southworth and Forbes (capt.); Barton, Dewar and Forrest; Lofthouse, Campbell, John Southworth, Walton and Townley. Sheffield Wednesday: Smith; Morley, Brayshaw; Dungworth, Betts, Waller; Ingram, Bennett, Mumford, Cawley and Woolhouse.

Just before the start a representative of "The Blackburn Times," on the alert for inside information, ran across Mr. R. P. Gregson, who had visited the dressing-rooms. "Who is going to win?" queried our reporter. "Oh," he replied, "Sheffield are beaten now!" "How do you make that out?" asked the journalist. "Well, I have just come from the dressing-rooms," was the answer. "The Wednesday are down in the dumps. They are as quiet as mice. They have not a word to say. They look frightened. But the Rovers are singing and whistling and carrying on like a lot of kittens. Unless I am very much mistaken they will win easily."

It was a remarkably accurate forecast, Sheffield, unnerved by the importance of the occasion, had a bad attack of stage fright, whereas their opponents entered the fray in jubilant spirits.. Forbes and his colleagues simply ran away with the Yorkshiremen, who were defeated to the tune of 6–1. Two records were established that memorable afternoon, The Rovers were the first club to collect half-a-dozen goals in the final (the previous highest being 3–0), and Townley covered himself with glory by scoring three of the goals.

At the interval the victors were leading 4–0. Subsequently they relaxed their efforts, and the Wednesday, after trying three times in succession to get past Forbes, made one more attempt, which succeeded, for when Ingram centred from the right, Mumford turned the ball past Horne. Townley registered the first, third and fifth goals for his side. He opened the Rovers' account by heading through a free kick taken by Forrest, and his second goal was obtained by a magnificent shot from near the corner-flag, the ball whizzing past the front of the nearest upright and close behind the second. Walton was responsible for the second goal, Jack Southworth for the fourth and Lofthouse for the sixth. Immediately after Lofthouse had steered the ball out of the reach of Smith the game was stopped for about five minutes, as the crowd broke into the enclosure and rushed for the grandstand, where preparations were being made for the presentation of the Cup and medals. Major Marindin, the referee, with the aid of police and soldiers, cleared the playing pitch and the contest was resumed, but nothing of note happened.

The Wednesday sportingly acknowledged that they were beaten on their merits. The "Blue and Whites," who took their magnificent victory very quietly, gave a grand display. Their forwards were excellent, Lofthouse, Townley, and Walton being the best of the five. Forrest and Dewar were the pick of the halves. Forbes was superb, and James Southworth revealed the qualities that gained him such honour and distinction in the semi-final. Horne had an easy passage, though he saved once in clever fashion when he was surrounded.

When the Cup winners arrived home at 10-30 the following

Monday night, they received a boisterous welcome from a mighty crowd. Preceded by a band, they were driven in a three-horse brake through the principal streets, amid deafening cheers. So dense was the throng that passage through it was only possible by a large body of police marching together in front of the band, whose appropriate airs included "See the conquering hero comes" and "Auld Lang Syne," the latter as a reminder that the trophy had previously been in Blackburn.

The next season the "Blue and Whites" once more distinguished themselves in the national Cup competition. They conquered Middlesbrough Ironopolis (3–0), Chester (7–0), Wolverhampton Wanderers (2–0), and West Bromwich Albion (3–2), with whom they had a keen duel in the semi-final. Their performances stamped them as a great team, though some of their supporters were under the impression that the Rovers would not do themselves justice in the final against Notts County, who, in fighting their way to the Oval, for the first time in their career, had knocked out Sheffield United (9–1), Burnley (2–1), Stoke (1–0), and met Sunderland in the semi-final, when each side scored three goals, necessitating another trial of skill, which terminated in favour of Notts by 2–0.

In view of the circumstance that the week before Notts County in a League match at Blackburn had defeated the Rovers 7–1, the outlook for the "Blue and Whites" was supposed to be none too hopeful. The faith of some of their supporters was so shaken that many absented themselves from the final because they had a rooted objection to "seeing their favourites beaten." They appeared to have forgotten that in the League contest the home side were not at full strength, and that Gow, in goal, had given a poor exhibition. The players, though, were not disheartened. They trained at home and prepared carefully for the momentous encounter at the Oval on March 21st, 1891.

So great was the demand for seats that people offered a guinea for a stand ticket, but had to be refused, as the accommodation was taxed to its utmost limit. The attendance reached 30,000, striking proof of the growing popularity of the pastime. At the last moment the Rovers had to make a change in their eleven. Harry Campbell, who had not been in the best of health, was taken suddenly ill. Consequently Combe Hall, formerly of St. Bernard's and known as the "Pocket Hercules," who had joined the club early in the season, was introduced at inside left, Walton crossing over to the right wing. Two other debutants were Rowland Pennington, a native of St. Helens, who had not figured in senior circles until he donned the blue and white jersey in October, 1890; and Tom Brandon, formerly of Paisley St. Mirren, who was disqualified from taking part in the later rounds of the Cup competition in 1890 through having participated in a football tournament in Scotland during the close season. The teams were :— Blackburn Rovers: R. Pennington; T. Brandon and J. Forbes (capt.); J. Barton, G. Dewar, and J. H. Forrest; J. Lofthouse, N. Walton, John Southworth. C. Hall and W. Townley. Notts County: J. Thraves, Ferguson and J. Hendry; A. Osborne, D. Calderhead and A. Shelton; T. McInnes. A. C. McGregor, J. Oswald. H. B. Daft and W. Locker.

All the gloomy forebodings entertained with respect to the "Blue and Whites" were falsified by the manner in which they comported themselves during a strenuous ordeal. They took the field as fit as fiddles, quietly confident of their ability and determined to uphold the glorious traditions of the club. Notts, too, were equally bent on winning. After a contest packed with thrilling incidents, victory rested with the Rovers by 3–1. Moreover, their success was thoroughly deserved. Their opponents, though disappointed that their hopes of Cup conquest had been extinguished, were the first to admit that they had been vanquished by a better side. The Rovers were the quicker on the ball, their combination was superior and their shooting was much more dangerous than that of their rivals. Their attack was well directed and sustained and their defence was above criticism. The soundness of the rearguard had an important bearing on the issue. If the backs had betrayed any weakness they would probably have been overwhelmed. Brandon and Forbes though were in magnificent form. They revelled in their work, seldom put a foot wrong, and by their skill and courage upset the calculations of the powerful Notts raiders. Behind them Pennington quite justified the confidence reposed in him. At centre-half Dewar played the game of his life.

Nine minutes from the start a throw-in, taken by Lofthouse near the corner flag, developed into a scrimmage in front of the County's goal, during which Thraves was beaten. The newspaper reports vary as to the actual scorer; the "Athletic News" credited Dewar with the point. Thirteen minutes later Southworth placed the Rovers further ahead with a pretty screw shot; and four minutes afterwards Townley headed a third goal. With this substantial lead the "Blue and Whites" crossed over. Their supremacy was not seriously challenged, though after 26 minutes in the second half Oswald succeeded in reducing the deficit.

"By their success," said the "Daily News," "the Blackburn team equalled the record of the once famous London Wanderers, who won the Cup five times during the first seven years of its existence. Indeed, without doing any injustice to the renowned amateur club, it may fairly be said, taking into consideration the enormous development of skill in Association football within the last few seasons, that the Rovers have accomplished the biggest performance in the history of English Association football." "Free Critic," in the "Athletic News," said: "If I were asked who won the match I should say Dewar, Brandon and Forbes."

A tremendous reception awaited the victors when they returned home the following Monday night, the demonstration almost equalling that given to the Olympic when they first brought the Association Cup to Lancashire. When captain Forbes, with the trophy in his possession, stepped from the train he was vociferously cheered. The players drove round the town in a wagonette drawn by five horses, with an outrider, preceded by the Blackburn Borough Band. Another conveyance, with six horses attached, contained officials. The streets were illuminated with coloured

F.A. CUP WINNERS, 1891.

STANDING : R. BIRTWISTLE (UMPIRE), T. BRANDON, R. PENNINGTON, J. BARTON, JOHN SOUTHWORTH, G. DEWAR, J. H. FORREST, E. MURRAY (TRAINER)
SITTING : J. M. LOFTHOUSE, N. WALTON, J. FORBES (CAPTAIN), COMBE HALL, W. TOWNLEY.

lights and scores of rockets were discharged in honour of the brilliant victory.

Among their other titles to fame, the "Blue and Whites" have a grand record in connection with the Lancashire Senior Cup competition. They have won this handsome trophy 11 times. Commencing with 1882 they were the victors for four years in succession. In the season 1900–1901 they encountered Bury, their old foe-men, in the second round. So equally were they matched that they had to meet five times to arrive at a definite result, the Rovers then winning 3–1. The first two ties were goalless, in the third each side scored thrice, and the fourth ended 1–1. Another dour contest was that with Burnley in the 1911 final. The sides drew three times (1–1, 2–2, 0–0) before the Rovers prevailed by 2–1. The following are their successes in the Lancashire Cup finals :—1882, beat Accrington, 3–1; 1883, Darwen, 3–2; 1884, Blackburn Olympic, 2–1 (after a draw, 1–1); 1885, Blackburn Olympic, 2–1; 1896, Bury, 2–0 (after a draw, 1–1); January, 1901, Burnley, 4–0; December, 1901, Burnley, 1–0; 1904, Southport Central, 2–1; 1906, Liverpool, 3–0; 1908, Liverpool, 5–3; 1911, Burnley, 2–1 (after three drawn games).

CHAPTER X. — ANOTHER NATIONAL RECORD.

Twelve Association Cup Semi-Finals — Rovers Create Another Record — Thrills at White Hart Lane — Blackpool's Challenge — Collapse Against Cardiff City — How "Blue and Whites" Fared from 1881 to 1925.

S TILL another national record was created by the Rovers last March when they reached the semi-final stage of the Association Cup competition for the twelfth time, or one more than Aston Villa. To obtain this distinction they played in seven matches in the four previous rounds. Oldham Athletic, for whom T. Heaton, the former Rover, appeared at centre-half, were beaten 1–0 at Ewood Park, McKay cleverly heading through from a corner taken by Hulme 25 minutes from the end. This solitary goal gave the "Blue and Whites" their first Association Cup victory at Blackburn since the war. Then followed three stern tussles with Portsmouth, in which neither side scored in the encounters at Ewood Park and Fratton Park, but at the third meeting, at Highbury, the Rovers prevailed, through a splendid solo effort by Crisp, who crowned a 35 yards dribble with a fast, rising shot that completely deceived the opposing custodian.

In the third round the "Blue and Whites," who now had the assistance of Puddefoot, their new centre-forward, nearly came to grief at White Hart Lane. With seven minutes to play Tottenham Hotspur enjoyed a lead of 2–0, but in an amazing finish the Lancastrians drew level and almost succeeded in winning. Hulme reduced the deficit with a dazzling shot, after which the 'Spurs were practically confined to their own territory. A minute from the end the Rovers were awarded a penalty. As Rollo was preparing to take the spot kick the referee consulted a linesman and then gave a goal-kick. Even that disheartening decision did not quench the ardour of the "Blue and Whites," who attacked so desperately that in the last few seconds of extra time allowed for stoppages McKay equalised during a scrimmage in the goalmouth. By their superb dash and courage the Rovers had accomplished the seemingly impossible, friend and foe alike cheering them to the echo. They made no mistake in the replay at Ewood Park, when their exhibition, easily the finest of the season, was worthy of the great eleven that wore the club's colours just before the war. Unlike their opponents, the Rovers wasted no time in manoeuvring on a heavy ground, but by sweeping advances, in which the point of attack was constantly changed, they gained a brilliant victory by 3–1. Campbell, Puddefoot and Hulme scored in the first half, and towards the finish Dimmock netted for the 'Spurs, who were run almost to a standstill. It was not until the home side relaxed their efforts that the visitors reproduced anything approaching their customary form.

Remarkable scenes were witnessed at Ewood Park on the occasion of the fourth round tie with Blackpool on March 7th. So great was the interest that an attendance of 60,011 set up a new record for the ground. Before and during the game members of the St. John Ambulance Brigade, who are on duty at all matches and whose services are highly appreciated, were busy conveying casualties, including stretcher cases, across the field to the recesses of the stand, where they received attention. The solid masses of spectators presented an inspiring sight. Some of them had gathered outside the enclosure soon after 9-00 a.m. At 1-30 there were 12,000 on the ground. Half-an-hour later the total had been increased to 40,000, and by 2-30 every entrance was closed. The top of the wall at the Blackburn end was lined with enthusiasts; others swarmed on to roofs of adjacent houses. That Blackpool's challenge was very real was evident from the start. The visitors

F.A. CUP SEMI-FINAL TEAM, 1889.

BACK ROW: JAMES SOUTHWORTH, H. ARTHUR, J. FORBES, W. TOWNLEY.
MIDDLE ROW: J. DOUGLAS, N. WALTON, W. ALMOND, J. H. FORREST.
FRONT ROW: R. HARESNAPE, JACK SOUTHWORTH (CAPTAIN), H. FECITT.

made no secret of their belief that, if they could hold the Rovers for half the game, they were capable of sharing the honours. While they accomplished the former—there were no goals at the interval—they over-estimated their ability in regard to the latter. Some 66 minutes had gone when the astuteness of McKay presented Puddefoot with a golden chance, which was promptly utilised. That successful shot settled the issue. Later the Blackburn centre-forward, after skilfully outwitting the backs, was so certain he had scored again that he wheeled to his left to return to the centre. The ball, however, struck the foot of the post to his right and rebounded into play. Both goals had thrilling escapes, and though the "Blue and Whites" were the more impressive team, Blackpool fought gamely to the end.

Thus for the first time since 1912 the Rovers qualified for the semi-final, with Cardiff City as their antagonists. Hopes ran high that the "Blue and Whites" would celebrate their golden jubilee as holders of the Cup. Those expectations were shattered when the elevens met on the Notts County ground at Meadow Lane on March 28th. A strong wind, a bouncing ball, defensive errors and the opportunism of the Welshmen caused a startling collapse of the favourites, who were three goals behind when play had been in progress 17 minutes. Hitherto the Blackburn rearguard had been noted for its assurance. On this great occasion it temporarily went to pieces, with disastrous consequences. The "Athletic News" described the debacle as "A tragedy in three acts." The first was when Rollo, attempting a hook clearance from a corner, turned the ball into the net after six minutes. Three minutes later he was again at fault, for he sliced a tricky bouncing ball, which soared into the air. As it came down Nicholson headed it to Gill, who had no difficulty in placing Cardiff further ahead. After 17 minutes Wylie failed to effectively check Davies. On the latter centreing Rollo and Sewell both advanced to take the ball; then each left it to the other, and during the brief pause Beadles darted between them to register City's third goal. In the last 11 minutes McKay headed through from a corner, but the Rovers were incapable of providing a stirring finish similar to that seen at White Hart Lane. They were a bitterly disappointed side, and the tragedy of the defeat lay in the fact that they had largely beaten themselves.

No fewer than 273,125 spectators attended the eight matches in which the "Blue and Whites" figured, the gross receipts being £20,500. The four ties played at Blackburn attracted 150,921 spectators, who paid £10,777 for admission, viz. : v. Oldham Athletic, attendance 24,531 and receipts £1,435; v. Portsmouth, 18,200 and £1,215; v. Tottenham Hotspur, 48,179 and £3,645; v. Blackpool, 60,011 and £4,482.

Cardiff City, making their first appearance in the final, were beaten 1–0 by Sheffield United, who won the trophy for the fourth time.

The gratifying progress in the national competition revives memories of the days when the "Blue and Whites" were supreme as Cup fighters. The club was virtually in its infancy when, in 1881-2, the contemporary football world was startled by the Rovers' extraordinary success in the Cup contests. By a series of notable performances they won their way to the final, in which, as recorded in an earlier chapter, they had to bow the knee to the Old Etonians. The following season, just when hopes were mounting again, Darwen beat them in a second round tie, in a great Derby match. But in 1883-4 the club made full amends. The side went through the earlier rounds like a whirlwind, scoring 27 goals prior to the semi-final. In that vigorous contest, at Birmingham, the "Blue and Whites" upset the calculations of Notts County, a much-fancied combination, and in the final vanquished Queen's Park, the glory of Scotland. By 5–1 they overwhelmed the Old Carthusians in the semi-final in 1884-5. That success caused a flutter in the dove-cotes, as their opponents included "the magnificent Cobbold," the brothers Walters and C. A. Smith. The Rovers crowned a brilliant season by retaining possession of the Cup, once more defeating Queen's Park in the final.

When the "Blue and Whites" completed the "hat trick" in 1886 they again asserted their superiority over the great amateur organisations of the south, for in the semi-final they defeated London Swifts (2–1), in whose ranks were such famous players as Lockhart-Mure, an extraordinary goalkeeper; Dr. Smith, the well-known Bambridge, and a trip of celebrated Corinthians in Brann, Saunders and Holden-White. On their third successive visit to the Oval the Lancastrians drew with West Bromwich Albion, but in the replay they conquered the Staffordshire eleven by two clear goals.

These were triumphs which set the seal on the Rovers' fame as wonderful Cup-tie players; but, strangely enough, the next year or two saw some decline in their power, two seasons passing without the club progressing further than the third round. But in 1888-9 the heights were touched. This was the period when the side scored 212 goals in their various matches, and locally it was firmly believed that the eleven would carry off the trophy once again. After Aston Villa had been thrashed 8–1 in the fourth round, it was expected Wolverhampton Wanderers would be subjected to the same fate in the semi-final. But the Midland club had other views. Playing with tremendous vigour, they first ran the Rovers to a draw at Crewe in a game which one critic described as "a dog-fight," and then beat them fairly and squarely by three goals to one in the replay, which the celebrated Major Marindin went to referee in person.

It was a bitter blow to Blackburn people. The following year, though, saw enthusiasm rekindled. The semi-final produced a great struggle. Wolverhampton made no secret of their belief in their ability to give the all- conquering Northerners a shock, and they went into the game with terrific zest. While the Rovers were the more skilful team, the Wolves' defence was rock-like, and the "Blue and Whites" only gained the day by a brilliant exploit by Jack Southworth. The famous centre-forward—some say he had not a peer—picked up a pass in mid-field and raced for goal on his own. He passed man after man, and shot just as he was knocked over, but the ball sped true to its mark. The final was more or less a picnic; Sheffield Wednesday were no match at all for the Rovers, who won as they pleased.

In this era the Rovers were redoubtable Cup-fighters, and

in 1890-91 they swept every team before them in their course to the semi-final, among others their old rivals, Wolverhampton Wanderers. The semi-final tie with West Bromwich Albion, at Stoke, produced an exciting struggle. In the early stages the Albion pressed very hard, and scored a fine goal. But the Blackburn men roused themselves with a vengeance, and after Jack Southworth had electrified the crowd with a brilliant goal, they played with irresistible spirit, gaining the verdict by 3–2. In the final the Rovers took the football world by storm by beating Notts County, as described in the preceding chapter.

West Bromwich made some amends by putting the Rovers out of the competition in the second round the following year. The "Blue and Whites," however, were irrepressible, and 1893 found them once again in the last four. After the inspiriting way the side had disposed of Sunderland in the previous round every confidence was felt in their ability to account for Wolverhampton Wanderers— it is singular how these two clubs came to be drawn against each other so frequently in those days—but pride was to have a great fall. Early in the game at Trent Bridge the Rovers recorded a pretty goal, but before long the Midland eleven equalised and went ahead before the interval. Though remarkable for its pace and keenness, the second half produced no goals. A critic, summing up the Rovers' display, said: "The defence was good enough, and the half-backs showed no weakness. But the forwards were inexpressibly feeble. Half the dash shown against Sunderland would have served. 'Tis human to err, however."

This falling-away in a department that had previously been very efficient was almost a kind of writing on the wall, in view of what the succeeding years were to bring. In 1894, it is true, the "Blue and Whites" revealed encouraging form in reaching the semi-final, and the general impression was that they would have no great difficulty in accounting for Notts County at Bramall Lane. But again the attack proved to have "temperament," and to the great disappointment of Blackburn enthusiasts the Rovers lost after having had three-parts of the game. To such straits did the attack decline that dashing Tom Brandon went to centre-forward near the end of this match, but his effort was unavailing. This was the beginning of a dismal period, all the more depressing because of previous glories, and in the span of the next seventeen years the Rovers did not progress further than the third round. Then an era dawned which was to bring fresh lustre to the old club. In 1911 the side put up a series of performances in the earlier rounds that generated terrific enthusiasm by the time the Rovers were to meet Bradford City in the semi-final. Many Blackburn people made the journey in high feather, only to return in chastened mood, as their favourites, who had been tipped throughout the length and breadth of the country as the potential Cup winners, were thoroughly well beaten by three goals to nothing. The main factor in that reverse was "nerves." The men never attained their normal form, with the result that Bradford City's dash and virility triumphed very easily. Though they had a strong breeze to help them in the first half, the Rovers were unable to drive home their advantage; while after the interval the Yorkshiremen scored twice within 13 minutes, which spelt disaster for their opponents. Again in 1912 the Rovers set their supporters' imagination on fire by the way they set about their pilgrimage to the semi-final. Norwich, Derby County and Wolverhampton Wanderers were disposed of handily. Then came the electrifying fourth round tie with Manchester United. The "Blue and Whites" first forced a draw at Old Trafford, and at Ewood Park pulled back a two-goals lead to win the replay during extra time, in one of the most sensational matches ever seen at Blackburn. Tremendous interest was taken in the semi-final tie with West Bromwich Albion, at Anfield. Unfortunately there was general trade depression at the time, and only a comparative handful of people were able to make the journey to Liverpool. The game, which ended in a draw, produced nothing out of the ordinary, save that in the second half Alfred Robinson, the Rovers' keeper, handled the ball only twice, so strongly did the game run in his team's favour. The replay on the Owlerton ground, Sheffield, was a curious affair in that the Rovers had all the game before the interval, and the Albion dominated matters afterwards, but neither could score, though once Shearman, the Albion winger, put a flag-kick into the Rovers' net without anyone touching the ball. When extra time began the Blackburn side's chances were strongly favoured, for they were a team with uncommon stamina; but to the dismay of their supporters, Robinson, who had given a wonderful exhibition of goalkeeping, was beaten by a short-range shot when only three minutes remained for play.

Thirteen years passed before the Rovers again appeared in a semi-final—last March. Though they were then denied the honour of making their debut at Wembley, they are to be heartily congratulated on their progress in the competition and on the new record they established.

CHAPTER XI. — TURBULENT SCENES AT EWOOD PARK.

Mob in Possession at Ewood Park — Darwen's Pride Affronted — Robert Crompton and Bob Haworth — Edgar Chadwick's Distinguished Career — Arnold Whittaker's Debut — Peter Somers and Hugh Morgan — A Surprise Packet from Scotland.

TURBULENT scenes occurred at Ewood Park during the festive season in 1890. For a while mob law held sway. A good deal of damage was done to the ground and fixtures, but fortunately there was little personal violence. The disturbance owed its inception to mistaken policy on the part of the Rovers' committee, who, without pondering over the possible consequences of their action, suddenly found themselves face to face with a serious situation. They had committed an error of judgment. In doing so they affronted Darwen's pride. The usual Christmas Day fixture with the Peaceful Valley club had been arranged. Mammoth posters on the hoardings had announced the match. Long-standing rivalry between the clubs ensured a large attendance. At the time advertised for the kick-off the spectators numbered not fewer than 3,000, quite half of whom were supporters of the visitors. The price of admission was 6d., stand and enclosure 1s., and reserved seats 1s. 6d.

Naturally it was expected that the Rovers would be represented by their premier eleven. To the disappointment and disgust of the crowd they relied on their second team, strengthened by Douglas, Almond and Fecitt. When they filed from the dressing-room their appearance was greeted with loud cries of dissent. Darwen's supporters appealed to their side not to leave the tent. The visitors, however, disregarded this advice. They were cheered on coming out, though a section of the crowd called on Joe Marsden to take his men off, which he did after they had been on the field scarcely a minute. This action caused much excitement. From the now thoroughly roused crowd there arose demands for the return of their money, expressed in the significant cry, "We haven't paid six-pence to see a second team match!"

Shortly afterwards Darwen paraded their second eleven. It was plain, though, that this expedient did not meet with the approval of the holiday crowd, who had gathered in expectation of seeing a keen contest. Events then moved rapidly. A spectator, presumably from Darwen, made his way on to the field. He was stopped by a police sergeant, but declined to go off. This open defiance of the law was instantly followed by thousands of people swarming on to the playing piece, compelling the teams to retire. As the small number of police in attendance were powerless to prevent the inrush of the yelling mob, pandemonium reigned supreme. Hostile elements, imprecating the Rovers, made a determined effort to force their way into the dressing tents. They would have succeeded in their fell design if it had not been for the foresight of the police, who, recognising that this was the real danger zone, stationed themselves in front of the door, where they formed an effective barrier.

The mob surged round the tent for a considerable time. Then it was announced that the match was abandoned and that pass-out checks would be issued for a future game. On receipt of this news about a third of the spectators went home, but 2,000 still remained, some bent on mischief. Tom Brandon was spotted near the grandstand. A cry of "Brandon's here!" was promptly raised. In the circumstance discretion was obviously the better part of valour, hence the full-back quickly made himself scarce.

Foiled in their intention of getting at the Rovers' players, the malcontents wreaked their vengeance on inanimate objects.

They pulled up the goalposts and smashed them, after which they invaded the grandstand, where they seized and tore to shreds the carpets on the reserved seats. Next they proceeded to a pay box, which they left without doing any damage. On passing the reporters' box it was suggested that "that greenhouse" should be demolished, but the habitation of the scribes was spared violation. A Rovers' official had his hat knocked off, and a stone was hurled through a window of the dressing rooms. As darkness fell and police reinforcements arrived, the crowd gradually dispersed, after spending a very exciting Christmas afternoon.

In commenting on this contretemps, "Veritas," in a letter to the Press, said the rumour had been afloat that the Rovers wished to cancel the fixture, owing to their engagement with Wolverhampton Wanderers the next day. He pointed out that "the Darwen committee had received no intimation to that effect and had journeyed to Blackburn under the impression that their side were to meet the Rovers' League team. At the last moment, however, it was found that the Rovers were playing their second team, and the Darwen men, accepting this as an insult, refused to play. It was then arranged that the Darwen Reserve and the Rovers' Reserve should play the match, and they appeared on the ground for this purpose. The spectators, however, could not see the force of this, and, breaking in, a general melee ensued." "Veritas" had no hesitation in apportioning the blame. "It will be seen," he said, "that the Rovers were altogether in fault." He expressed the view that if the Rovers had notified Darwen that they desired to cancel the fixture or intended it for reserve teams the Darwen committee would doubtless have obliged them, and he added, "Fortunately, such exhibitions as that seen at Ewood, which are highly reprehensible, are of rare occurrence."

In the League tournament the "Blue and Whites," after their providential escape from the Second Division in 1897-8, showed considerable improvement. The side was reorganised, the Scottish element being singularly small. Geordie Anderson, who again threw in his lot with the club, not only filled his own position adequately, but rendered valuable service in tutoring the forwards. New men in the attack included Williams, of Everton, Wilson, of Swindon, and Moreland. Robert Crompton, who had been signed in September, 1896, as a "very promising youth, who has played for the Trinity Club," now came rapidly to the front, as did Bob Haworth, another local product, who figured in the intermediate line. Crompton was a tower of strength in the rear division, and Haworth, although only a stripling, made a reputation at centre-half, after Anderson had once more departed to New Brighton. Tom Booth, who is now among the amateur billiards champions of the country; Chambers (Workington) and Houlker acquitted themselves with credit as half-backs; while of the forwards Briercliffe, Williams, Evans, Hulse, Jackson, Blackburn, Hurst (Workington) and Moreland helped to register notable victories.

After an opening reverse of 2–1 at Everton, the team had a remarkable run of success, and for a short time had the distinction of heading the League table. From October they did not fare so well until the new year, when they again came into prominence, eventually finishing sixth, with 36 points. Of their 14 victories nine were recorded at Blackburn, while on tour they accounted for Nottingham Forest, Sheffield Wednesday, Bolton Wanderers, Stoke and Sunderland. On appearing at Nottingham (September 3rd, 1898) they had the honour of assisting at the opening of the Forest's new ground at Trent Bridge, on which £13,000 had been expended. It was expected that the Forest, who were the holders of the Association Cup, would worthily celebrate the auspicious event, but to the surprise of their supporters they were beaten 1–0, Jackson scoring seven minutes from the end. This was Crompton's first game of the season as Brandon's partner, and he fully justified the confidence reposed in him.

A kinematograph record was taken of the Rovers' signal triumph over West Bromwich Albion at Ewood Park on September 24th, 1898, when the visitors were vanquished 4–1. Many who were present have not yet forgotten the great game in which the "Blue and Whites" defeated Sunderland at Blackburn by the odd

ROBERT CROMPTON.

Holds English International record with 34 caps. Famous captain and brilliant right back. Connected with Blackburn Rovers during the whole of his playing career of 24 years; now a director of the club. One of the greatest figures in Association Football.

goal in five. It was a Titanic struggle. Both teams played brilliantly, and the issue hung in the balance right up to the last second. Carter, the home custodian, was in wonderful form. With the Wearsiders striving their utmost to secure an equaliser, he stopped a hot shot by throwing himself on the ball, which he hugged in the midst of a writhing mass of players. By an extraordinary effort he managed to raise himself and fling the ball over his head down the field. Carter's pluck saved a certain goal, and his clearance was little short of marvellous. Among other achievements the "Blue and Whites" netted three times in the first ten minutes against Newcastle United at Ewood, and on the same ground scored six goals against Notts County.

Quite unexpectedly three successive reverses were sustained in the October-November period. Rumour became busy. All kinds of tales were bandied about. For instance, it was alleged that the team were suffering from discontent, also that the treatment of Killean had given rise to much dissatisfaction. That player was injured in a test match the previous April, was not signed for the ensuing season, and in November, 1898, it was reported that he had migrated to Glossop North End. In view of the prevalence of these alarmist rumours, the directors discussed the matter early in December, and then had a meeting with the players, at which Geordie Anderson, the captain, declared that there was no foundation for the allegations. With respect to Killean, it was pointed out that he had suffered no injustice at the hands of the club.

From the beginning of June to the early part of September he had been in receipt of a weekly allowance, although the club's liability in regard to him ended with the close season. He had been placed under the care of the club's doctor, and when he was reported fit for football the Rovers offered him a short engagement to see if his injured limb would stand the strain. If so, they were prepared to engage him for the remainder of the season. These conditions were accepted by Killean, the trial was satisfactory, but when it came to re-signing the parties could not agree on terms, consequently the player was transferred to Glossop. The publication of this information cleared the air, and as the team struck a winning vein the ridiculous stories, which seldom contain even an atom of truth, but which are nearly always resurrected when a side happen to be down on their luck, faded into oblivion.

During the spring the wedding took place at Westbury Church of Mr. J. C. H. Bowdler, of Shrewsbury, formerly a playing member of Wolverhampton Wanderers and Blackburn Rovers and an international several times capped by Wales. A dashing forward, he was a genuine flyer, and often electrified spectators by his brilliance. Charlie Bowdler played particularly well in the season 1892-3, and gave an exhilarating display against Sunderland in the third round of the Association Cup competition at Ewood Park in February, 1893, when the Blackburn eleven won 3–0 before 28,000 spectators. His brother was also a popular wearer of the blue and white jersey. At the time he was married, Mr. Bowdler occupied the position of chairman of Shrewsbury Town F.C., and rendered valuable service to the game in which as an exponent he was a shining light. He still takes great interest in the winter pastime.

There was no angling after stars for the season 1899-1900, and though the Rovers did not cut much ice in the League, some of the young players they had enlisted showed much promise. Carter, Chambers and Moreland had departed. Anderson, who seemed as if he could not stay long away from Blackburn, reappeared, and Arthur Blackburn, having benefited by his experience with Southampton, again donned the blue and white jersey. He had developed into a fine defender, cool in emergencies, with plenty of power in his volleying. Of the recruits Arnold Whittaker, from Accrington Stanley, was a real capture, and Crook, late of Stalybridge Rovers, was another useful forward. Thompson, who had given evidence of ability on being promoted from the second team towards the end of the previous season, was further tested in goal, but as he did not maintain his early promise he was supplanted by Knowles, who had the veteran Brandon and the youthful

Crompton in front of him. The old Paisley St. Mirren defender, after rendering conspicuous service to the side, revealed signs of wear and tear as the season advanced. Ultimately he was dropped, and later returned to Scotland. On the other hand, Crompton gained in power and prestige. The vacancy in the rear division was allotted to A. Hardy, an adept at both cricket and football. During the previous summer he had acted as professional for Wigan C.C., and in the winter had played for Wigan County, being regarded as one of the best left-backs in the Lancashire League.

Edgar Chadwick, once of the Olympic and the Rovers, was the master mind of the Burnley attack that defeated the "Blue and Whites" 1–0 at Turf Moor in October, 1899, on which occasion Geordie Anderson was at outside-right for Blackburn. Though the visitors held the upper hand in the first half, they failed at close quarters. After the interval Burnley reversed the roles; but they, too, did not shine in front of goal. Chadwick, though, was for ever scheming to outwit the Blackburn defence. Twice he hit an upright, and it was through his efforts that Burnley obtained the goal that spelt victory. Originally a half-back, this brilliant exponent joined the Rovers in the 'eighties, and was transferred to inside-left, where he became a star artiste. When payment of wages was legalised he received 30s. a week, and as an application for an advance was turned down he left for Everton, with whom he had a distinguished career. Subsequently he assisted Burnley, Southampton, Liverpool, Blackpool, Glossop and Darwen. His honours include seven internationals, in which he appeared five times against Scotland. It used to be a commonplace in the descriptive accounts of his day to say "Chadwick seemed to have the ball tied to his toe." Some of his colleagues declared that he could dribble the ball round the edge of a threepenny-bit. He belonged to the golden age of the game, when footballers were artistes and craftsmen. There have been few men so packed with guile as this genial, unassuming little man, whose association with Milward, of Everton, set up one of the classic partnerships in football history. During the war period, when the Rovers were hard pressed for players, owing to military necessities, Chadwick made a picturesque reappearance at Ewood Park in November, 1916, playing at inside-left against Manchester United, who won 2–1. While the passing of time had not dimmed his enthusiasm it had robbed him of his pace, and he discovered that it was not easy for a veteran to "come back" after nine years' absence from regular participation in football. At the same time he willingly helped the club out of a difficulty, and received a very cordial reception.

Arnold Whittaker signalised his debut with the League eleven by performing the "hat trick" against North End at Ewood Park on October 14th, 1899. All the goals, the only ones scored in the match, were obtained in the first half. Whittaker's sparkling display aroused the enthusiasm of 10,000 spectators. McBride, who was under the bar for the visitors, came in for a round of hooting for the way in which he treated the debutant. He had cleared his goal when the Rovers' inside-right ran close to him. The Preston custodian had evidently lost his temper, for he seized Whittaker by the neck and gave him a good shaking. The crowd, amazed at the unrehearsed incident, did not forget to let McBride know what they thought of his childish conduct. Luckily for the offender the referee did not witness the act, so he escaped the consequences of his unsportsmanlike behaviour. On the same occasion, Dewhurst, a Padiham product, made his initial appearance in first-class company, leading the attack in a manner that won the commendation of the critics. He was entitled to some of the credit attaching to Whittaker's goals, and had hard lines in not scoring on his own account.

The following week the "Blue and Whites" surrendered two points to Nottingham Forest at Trent Bridge. Quarter of an hour from the end their opponents enjoyed a lead of three clear goals, but in a grand finish the Rovers scored twice and nearly equalised. The football during that closing period was of the most exciting description. The Forest were hemmed in their own territory, and the plucky rally of the Blackburn visitors earned unstinted admiration. Though they lost seven of their first ten matches, the side were nevertheless capable of giving an excellent account of themselves, as Everton discovered when they came to Blackburn late in November. The ultimate defence was as usual—Knowles, Brandon and Crompton—but Swift was introduced at right-half, Booth and Haworth completing the line. Dewhurst was restored as centre-forward vice Hulse, who was moved to inside-right, with Briercliffe as his partner, instead of Anderson, and the left flank consisted of F. Blackburn and Hurst. The changes had a stimulating effect. A substantial victory of 3–1 was quite refreshing, and did something to increase the confidence of the Ewood supporters.

Tom Briercliffe, "Chip" to everybody, was one of the most effective wingers of his day, and though he never actually won a "cap," he was reserve in a North v. South game, and reserve in an international match with Ireland. Strong and clever, he began his playing career with St. Luke's Juniors, and before donning the Rovers' colours in 1897 earned a name for himself, while only 17, with Wheelton and Clitheroe. While with the last-named he figured in the Rest of the League side v. Chorley, the then champions of the Lancashire Combination. It is interesting to note that the Rovers obtained his signature while he was recovering from a broken collar-bone, so keen were they to have his services. He performed excellently with the "Blue and Whites" for three seasons. "Chip" took part in the first two games of the twice replayed Cup-tie with Portsmouth in 1900, an injury in the second match accounting for his absence at the final meeting. On leaving Ewood he assisted Stalybridge for a short period, and then earned more laurels with Woolwich Arsenal and Plymouth Argyle, appearing in a match styled London v. Sheffield while with the former, and Devonshire v. Cornwall while with the seaport eleven. He was a member of the Woolwich side which won promotion to the First Division. "Chip" played a leading part in that achievement, for, in addition to giving fine displays on the wing, he scored no fewer than eighteen goals from outside-right. After a career on the playing-field of over fifteen years, he retired from the game when Brentford were angling for his services. He still resides in Blackburn and takes a keen interest in the "Blue and Whites."

Photo by W. Bolton, Blackburn

F. BLACKBURN.

T. BRIERCLIFFE.

ARNOLD WHITTAKER.

H. CHIPPENDALE.

There was great jubilation when the Ewood side registered their first League success over Bury, who had often checked their aspirations. It was on December 16th, 1899, at Blackburn, that this memorable event was chronicled. Bury, unbeaten for six weeks, put up a great fight. They scored twice in the first half without response by the Rovers. Not only so, but they defended so stubbornly after Haworth had reduced the deficit that it looked as if history would repeat itself. Believing that the "Blue and Whites" were engaged in a hopeless struggle, many spectators left the ground. Later they repented their precipitancy. However desperate their situation the Rovers never exhibited the white flag. At Nottingham and elsewhere they had furnished proofs of their courage, allied with staying power. They had old scores to wipe out against Bury. Hence with unflinching ardour they attacked again and again. Though often repulsed they declined to yield. Their reward came six minutes from the finish, when Blackburn, slipping between the backs, had the ball in the net in a twinkling, and with but three minutes to play Hulse scored the winning goal. Every man on the home side was a thorough trier. None, though, did better than Anderson, who was back in the intermediate line, where he was of greater service than as a forward. That season Bury had the honour of winning the Association Cup, vanquishing Southampton 4–0, and the following Wednesday they had their revenge on the "Blue and Whites," whom they defeated 2–0 at Gigg Lane.

A scene occurred at Ewood Park early in January, 1900. A blizzard was raging. Sheffield United were the visitors. When the game had been in progress 25 minutes, Mr. Scragg, the referee, consulted the linesmen, evidently being of opinion that football was out of the question. The spectators, though, clamoured for the game to continue. Eleven minutes later a player, who had collided with an opponent, had to be assisted to the pavilion. He was thoroughly exhausted. As the other men were chilled to the bone the referee abandoned the match, and the players gladly sought shelter. This decision did not please a section of the crowd, who noisily demonstrated in front of the dressing tents, where a part of the barrier was demolished. The rougher element rushed to the grandstand, picked up the carpets and threw them into the mud. Their hooliganism, however, terminated when additional police, summoned by telephone, suddenly appeared on the ground, which they speedily cleared.

It was in this season that the Rovers and North End first encountered each other in the Association Cup competition. On the date originally fixed (February 10th, 1900), play was impossible owing to a snowstorm, so the sides met a week later at Deepdale, before 14,000 spectators, who paid £441 for admission. The Rovers were represented by Knowles; Brandon, Crompton; Haworth, Booth, Houlker; Whittaker, Hulse, Dewhurst, Blackburn and Hurst. A stiff tussle, full of excitement, was anticipated. In this respect the spectators were not disappointed. Interest in the play never flagged. A goal by Henderson in the last five minutes—the only one scored—enabled Preston to pass into the next round. On this afternoon the Rovers were the victims of misfortune, as early in the game Hulse was injured and became practically a passenger. Despite this handicap the losers were undeniably the better team.

Hereabouts the defence was strengthened by the custodianship of Walter Whittaker, a native of Manchester, who had played for Fairfield, Newton Heath, Grimsby and Reading. Though he had his off days, he gave many brilliant exhibitions as a wearer of the blue and white colours. Peter Somers, who was born at Motherwell, and had seen service with Hamilton Athletic and Glasgow Celtic, was also a valuable asset. A brainy and astute inside-right, he was not only a skilful individualist, but his ability was freely placed at the disposal of his colleagues. In this Scot the fearless and dashing Whittaker found a cool and calculating partner. The blending of their qualities created a great wing. When Somers arrived the fortunes of the Rovers were at a low ebb. His presence had a revivifying influence. Much anxiety, however, was felt during the closing weeks of the campaign, because ground previously lost was difficult to recover. But the men were imbued with the right spirit, shown by the fact that in their last 13 League fixtures they gained 15 invaluable points, including a victory over Notts County in a vital match on April 28th. Two days later they visited Deepdale. North End's fate then hung in the balance, as a defeat meant relegation. However, Preston rose to the occasion, winning 2–0. It was a thrilling finish to a hard season. Although their position had been insecure, the Rovers' spirited football in the last two months increased their points to 30, which placed them 13th in the list, or five from the bottom.

High-class football, with little to choose between most of the sides, was a conspicuous feature of the League contests the following season (1900-1901). Liverpool carried off the championship with 45 points, Sunderland were runners-up with 43, and Notts County third with 40. The Rovers, with 33 points, were a creditable ninth. The eleven had undergone many changes. Brandon was an absentee, Booth had accepted an offer from Everton, Briercliffe had removed to Stalybridge, and Anderson, Hulse, Hurst, and Crook had also found fresh quarters. Their successors included James Moir, a youthful half-back from Glasgow Celtic; Hugh Morgan, formerly of Paisley St. Mirren and Liverpool, who had established a reputation as an inside-left; and W. Bryant, late of Newton Heath, who could not get a constant position in the side owing to the success of A. Whittaker, but when he was included showed himself to be a fast and skilful forward. Bryant, who was not afraid to take any berth, deputised so efficiently as leader of the attack at Birmingham that he scored three goals, thus enabling the Rovers to share the spoils.

Of a group of players from Reading, Walter Whittaker was the golden nugget, O'Brien, Hosie and Kelly not securing regular places in the senior team. Moir was a surprise packet. As next to nothing was known of him locally, he was regarded as a negligible quantity, but he astonished the club's supporters by demonstrating in the practice matches that his knowledge of half-back play was far superior to that of any of the recruits engaged for the intermediate line. So satisfactory was his form that the directors had no hesitation in selecting him to do duty with the seniors. They had no reason to regret their choice. Houlker, probably the most consistent member of the side the previous season, again played finely. Haworth impressed at centre-half, and McClure was sturdy and useful in the intermediate line. Crompton's value became more and more apparent. He was a magnificent defender, and had a worthy partner in Hardy. Dewhurst, a much-improved centre-forward, who had outrivalled Oldham, formerly of Everton, for the leadership, had an artiste on either side of him in Morgan and Somers. Several clubs cast longing eyes on Fred Blackburn, who had taken part in his first international and had scored one of the goals that permitted England to draw with Scotland at the Crystal Palace. Although tempting offers came his way, he elected to remain at Ewood, a decision that gave much satisfaction to all interested in the "Blue and Whites."

SEASON 1900-1901.

STANDING : J. WALMSLEY (SECRETARY), R. CROMPTON, J. MOIR, WALTER WHITTAKER, R. HAWORTH, A. HARDY,
N. WALTON (TRAINER), A. E. HOULKER.
SITTING : ARNOLD WHITTAKER, P. SOMERS, J. DEWHURST, W. BRYANT, F. BLACKBURN.

CHAPTER XII. — BOLD BID FOR LEAGUE HONOURS.

Features of a Strenuous Campaign — Albert Houlker's Grit — Cowell's Duels with Welsh Wizard — "Tinker" Davies' Amazing Scoring — Scribe's Left-handed Tribute to Crompton — John Simpson's Skill and Popularity.

APART from the fact that they finished third in the second season, the Rovers did not do anything exceptional in the League until 1901-2, when they made a bold bid for the chief honours. However, when their hopes were brightest an unexpected defeat by Sunderland at Ewood Park ruined their prospects, and though at one time they were second on the list they finished fourth. The Wearsiders carried off the championship with 44 points. Everton were second with 41, Newcastle United third with 37, and the Rovers next with 36. The natural disappointment of the "Blue and Whites" was tempered by the knowledge that during a strenuous campaign they had been responsible for football in which science, dash, pluck and enthusiasm were characteristic features. Dewhurst was the chief Blackburn marksman, with 18 goals to his credit out of the 52 registered by the team (only Everton, with 53, exceeding this number). Fred Blackburn performed so successfully on the left wing that he gained his second cap, this time against Ireland. In 1901 he had played against Scotland, and a similar honour was conferred on him in 1904.

Albert Houlker, who still lives in his native Blackburn, where he enjoys well-deserved popularity, was a demon for work in the intermediate line. His undoubted skill earned him the first of the five international caps that he now possesses, and the recognition was the more flattering because he displaced Ernest Needham, of Sheffield United, in the great match against Scotland, at Glasgow. Quick as a terrier, neat and nippy, Houlker when in action was the embodiment of perpetual motion. His heart was in the game. If he missed a shot he thumped himself in vexation, but when he scored a point he flung up his arms in joy. In an international against Ireland the Belfast crowd could scarcely believe he was not a son of Erin. They were delighted with his picturesque football, and their sentiments were voiced by an enthusiast who exclaimed: "Ye'r the broth of a boy, and sure it is ye'r Oirish!" "Kelly" was a great favourite wherever he went. Portsmouth, Southampton and Colne are among the clubs who retain pleasing recollections of the grit and sportsmanship of this grand half-back. Old memories were revived by his reappearance at Ewood Park in January, 1918. For half-a-dozen years he had been out of the game, and it was only the fact that he thought he might be able to render a service to the harassed Rovers that induced him to again don the old colours. It was no light undertaking for a man of his age to compete with athletes who were learning history and geography when he was a member of England's intermediate line. Houlker, however, placed his reputation on the knees of the gods. It is no exaggeration to say he played a great game, a wonderful game, under the circumstances, and was fresher at the finish than some of his colleagues who had been appearing regularly. Few who witnessed his display will forget his triumphant return to the scene of his former conquests.

Crompton was unquestionably the finest player in the Ewood side, of which he had been appointed captain, and in which Somers, McClure, Morgan and Arnold Whittaker continued to be shining lights. It was in this season that Crompton began his brilliant international career, carrying all before him.

In view of these performances it was confidently expected that the Rovers' League stock would steadily soar, but as it turned out the opposite was the case. Three disastrous years followed, during which the "Blue and Whites" appeared incapable of doing themselves justice, especially in attack, the weakness of the forwards in front of goal being the principal stumbling-block. R. O. Evans, formerly of Wrexham and Coventry City, one of the finest goalkeepers in the four countries, who was honoured by Wales on 10 occasions, gave superb displays under the bar. His consistency made him one of the idols of the public. Towards the close of the season in 1904 he had the misfortune to strain a knee, which kept him out of the field for six weeks. With more or less success, efforts were made to find a capable partner for Crompton, whose services to the club during this anxious period cannot be overestimated. The form of Jack Eastham, the Blackburn youth, became so uncertain that he was dropped in favour of Riley, late of Chorley, who eventually was superseded by Jack Cameron, of Scottish fame. Among the half-backs W. Bradshaw, a nugget picked up from Accrington Stanley, was steadily gaining in favour. McClure, when he curbed a tendency to roam, was effective, while Sam Wolstenholme, who hailed from Little Lever, and had assisted Farnworth Alliance and Horwich prior to winning his spurs with Everton, distributed the ball with rare judgment, but the forwards, generally speaking, did not make the best use of the openings he provided. Moir was rarely off form and sometimes approached brilliance. A. Whittaker and Adam Bowman, who showed his colleagues how to shoot, both did well in the front line.

It almost seemed, indeed, as if the Rovers, who were perilously near relegation in 1898, were destined to sink into the Second Division. Happily, such a calamity was averted. At the same time their supporters approached the season 1905-6 with misgiving. The "Blue and Whites," though, proved the truth of the old adage that "it is a long lane that has no turning." For three years in succession they had been under a cloud. Now they came out in their true colours and performed so well that it was thought they would annex the championship. They did not succeed in reaching the top rung of the ladder, but they earned more points (40) than ever before. Arthur Cowell, introduced at left-back, developed wonderfully under the tuition of such a craftsman as Crompton, and laid the foundation of his highly-successful career. Prior to joining Nelson, from whom he went to Ewood, this Blackburn youth played for St. Peter's in the local Sunday School League, with which Crompton, Whittaker, Miles Chadwick, Jack Eastham and other Rovers were associated in their early days. What he lacked in inches Cowell made up in skill and pertinacity. He was a polished and accomplished defender, with splendid judgment, and could manoeuvre in the smallest possible space. It was always a treat to see Cowell and Billy Meredith in opposition. The famous Welsh international was seldom happy against the plucky little left-back of the Rovers, who so cleverly pitted his skill against the wizardry of his great antagonist, and the keen duels between the pair were worth going a long way to witness. Cowell's merits certainly deserved more than one international cap. In November the side were deprived of the services of their able centre-half, Jack Birchall, formerly of Blackpool, whose feeding, tackling and screw shots were alike excellent. To the deep regret of his colleagues he broke a leg at Sheffield, and his absence was deplored by the team. Towards the close of the season Arthur Dawson, who also achieved distinction as a cricketer with Rishton and East Lancashire, in the Lancashire League, played regularly at outside left with the first eleven. He knew how to centre when on the run, was a dependable shot, and generally rendered excellent service.

"Tinker" Davies, the lion-hearted Welshman, was now the pivot. He performed amazing feats as a dribbler, often crowning thrilling runs with goals that caused crowds to roar themselves hoarse with joy. As examples of his brilliance, it may be mentioned that he twice registered four goals in a match for the "Blue and Whites" in one season. The first occasion was in November, 1908, when his magnificent achievement electrified the Goodison Park spectators, who had counted on victory, seeing that Everton were leading by three goals with only 20 minutes to play, but when the whistle went the score stood four each! The following April at Bristol he repeated his exploit by netting all the goals

Season 1903-1904.

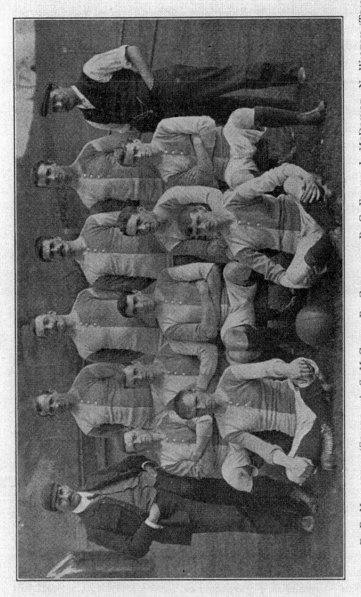

Standing: R. B. Middleton (Secretary), S. McClure, R. Crompton, R. O. Evans, J. McDonald, N. Walton (Trainer).
Middle Row: A. Whittaker, G. Smith, A. Bowman, L. Watson, F. Blackburn.
In Front: J. Dewhurst, W. Bradshaw.

obtained by his side, City being beaten 4–1. Davies took part in eleven internationals for Wales, appearing three times against both England and Scotland; and would have been more frequently capped if he had not met with so many accidents. Born at Wrexham, he joined a junior club called Wrexham Victoria; while with this organisation he was signed by Wrexham as a centre-half, but a vacancy occurring in the front line, he was tried as the leader. His success was instantaneous; he had an unquenchable thirst for goals. In his first match at Ewood towards the end of the 1905 season he scored three goals for the Reserve against Earlstown. A compatriot was so elated by the debutant's prowess that he rushed into the Press box and implored a representative of "The Blackburn Times" to despatch the following telegram to Wrexham: "Tinker scored three times. Twice put goalkeeper in net!" That was how "Tinker" played throughout the whole of his career. He was second to none in dash and ability.

A series of mishaps to players told its tale in 1906-7, when the old club had to struggle hard to save its reputation. Inconsistency was the bane. Yet when the position was so critical the men redeemed themselves by collecting a priceless seven points in the last four games. That opportune revival enabled them to finish twelfth from the top and eighth from the bottom, While Evans' star was on the wane, McIvor proved himself a first-class custodian. Though the smallest goalkeeper in the League, he was wonderfully expert and reliable, parrying high and low drives with equal facility. Jack Cameron, at full-back, silenced his critics by the soundness of his football, but as he could not secure a regular position in the eleven, owing to the superior claims of Cowell, he went to Chelsea in October, 1907. Tommy Suttie, who accepted the hardest knocks with smiling composure, was a new-comer. He had previously helped Leith to win the championship of the Second Division of the Scottish League. If his methods were somewhat unorthodox, there was no mistaking his zeal and energy. On making his appearance at outside left, E. Bracegirdle, from Knutsford, by his speed and dexterity gave promise of a bright future, but as he did not quite approximate to First League standard he was transferred in 1911 to Crewe Alexandra. In a military match during the war Bracegirdle registered six of the seven goals obtained by the Shropshire Light Infantry against The King's Regiment. Martin, who had a very successful season, recording no fewer than 27 of the 78 goals secured by the Rovers in the League and various cup ties, developed the curious habit of turning his back on his opponents' charge, and was fond of tracing circles with the ball. If it had not been for these mannerisms he would probably have found the net on many more occasions.

A lean time was experienced the following winter. The "Blue and Whites" were reduced to such straits that it was not until three points were gained out of two away engagements towards the close of the campaign that the club was assured of continuance in the premier division. In the hope of effecting an improvement, Anthony, Wombwell, W. Cameron and Kyle were added to the playing staff. Cameron, who was a polished footballer, was transformed into the utility man of the side. He could play anywhere, and occupied so many different positions that he would not have been surprised if he had been asked to do duty under the bar. A thorough Scot, he was identified with Albion Rovers and Renton before crossing the Border in 1904 to wear successively the Glossop and Bolton Wanderers' colours. Then he came to Blackburn, subsequently going to Hull City and Bury, and in 1919 he was appointed secretary-manager of the last-named club.

The advent of an international goalkeeper in the person of J. Ashcroft, late of Woolwich Arsenal, coincided with a phenomenal season, opening in September, 1908. The Rovers were now on the upgrade, but were still a puzzling combination. In fact, their form that winter was one of the curiosities of sport. On tour they were well-nigh invincible, but at home their repeated failures were inexplicable. Still, they gathered 41 points, or one above their previous best, which entitled them to the fourth place in the League. Geo. Chapman, an unknown quantity at the beginning of the tournament, was a dominant figure at centre-half. The previous season he was with Raith Rovers, and before then with Heart of Midlothian, with whom, however, he could not gain his proper position owing to it being occupied by the well-known Charlie Thomson. Bradshaw and Albert Walmsley were able coadjutors. Davies had a splendid season, scoring 19 times, with "Eddie" Latheron, one of the best inside-forwards the club has ever possessed, second on the list with 10 goals. Ellis Crompton obliged with nine and Kyle with eight. In the rout of Sunderland at Ewood, to the tune of 8–1, W. Garbutt, the new outside-right, had a hand in all the home goals. Born at Stockport, he had been with Reading and Woolwich Arsenal. He was a beautiful performer, and keeping the ball close to his feet, was an adept dribbler, from whose accurate low centres many goals were registered. With Holley (Sunderland) as his partner, Garbutt gave a meritorious display in an Inter-League match at Blackburn, in February, 1910, when Scotland beat England 3–2.

The coveted championship was almost within the grasp of the Rovers in 1909-10. From towards the close of October to the first week in January, with the exception of a few days, they held the leadership. Then ill-luck in the shape of accidents and a slump in play upset their calculations, and, despite a gallant effort, the leeway could not be restored. Eight months' unceasing endeavour gave them third position in the table, with 45 points, so that they were getting nearer to the realisation of their ambition. A tit-bit of the season was a sporting scribe's comment, after the international with Scotland, that "a long list of honours seems to be weighing heavily on the Rovers' captain." Doubtless the Scots, who never made the mistake of underrating his ability, would have been glad from a national standpoint if Crompton had been superseded, but for the next four years their forwards had to meet his unflinching opposition.

That the directors were desirous of building a first-class team was shown by the progressive policy which resulted in John Simpson, of Falkirk, crossing the Border, an event that aroused widespread interest. The transfer fee was understood to be £1,850.

The famous winger, who was born at Pendleton, Manchester, while his mother was on a short visit to Lancashire, returned to Scotland as a babe and lived at Laurieston until he came to Blackburn. His first appearance in English League football was on the Sheffield United ground on January 28th, 1911. Robert Benson, taking his benefit that day, profited accordingly, for he received £680, which was twice as much as he expected. Simpson, as modest as he was clever, was a magnet wherever he went. He rendered yeoman service to the side until a breakdown in health necessitated his retirement from the game. His popularity ranked with that of princes. Hundreds of thousands of spectators flocked to see him play. He was a miracle worker on the field, and so consummate was his skill that from almost any position and using either foot he could direct the ball with unerring accuracy towards goal. "Joe" Clennel, who sprang to the front with a bound with Blackpool, was another recruit who imparted increased striking power to the attack.

CHAPTER XIII. — LEAGUE CHAMPIONS.

Radiant Deeds — League Champions Twice in Three Years — Unbeaten at Home — The "Golden Wing" — Directors' Bold Policy Justified by Results — Dawson's Spectacular Performances — Chapman's Glorious Goal Against Manchester United.

AFTER much tribulation the "Blue and Whites" had arrived at last at what can truthfully be described as a glorious epoch in their League history. Twice within the next three years they had their names inscribed as champions on the imperishable scroll of fame. Their radiant deeds were comparable to those of the giants of the past. Indeed, there are some who contend that pride of place in the League confers greater renown than winning the F.A. Cup. Crompton, their illustrious captain, had the proud satisfaction of leading them to victory after victory until their triumph was assured. Thus at the end of April, 1912, the Rovers were hailed as champions for the first time in their career. Their points totalled 49, as against 46 for Everton and 44 for Newcastle United, second and third respectively. They won 20 and drew 9 of the 38 games, scoring 60 goals against 43. "Watty" Aitkenhead, operating chiefly at inside-left, had the distinction of registering 15 of the goals. Chapman, Clennel and Orr had nine apiece, and Latheron seven. As neither Aitkenhead nor Davies adequately filled the role of pivot, and as various experiments did not solve the problem, Chapman was moved to centre-forward as a last resort, and by his splendid pace, dash and opportunism largely contributed to the success of the side. As befitted a man of his reputation, Simpson was a star performer, and Anthony at outside-left gave of his best. The defence, in which the agile and daring Robinson had succeeded Ashcroft, was nothing short of brilliant. Walmsley, Smith and Bradshaw scintillated as an intermediate trio, while further behind Robinson, Crompton and Cowell were a magnificent rearguard, with a perfect understanding of each other's methods.

So finely did the team play that they went through the season without sustaining a single League reverse at Ewood Park, thus repeating the achievement of the campaigns of 1888-89 and 1909-10. At home they won 13 and drew 6 matches. Their away record was not as flattering, for they lost more games on tour than they won (seven victories against nine defeats), drawing the other three. It is singular that in few of these 38 games was the scoring of a sensational character. On the other hand, so powerful was the defence that in 14 of the matches not a goal was registered against the "Blue and Whites," whereas their forwards failed to score on but eight occasions. The most impressive victory was by four clear goals against Woolwich Arsenal at Blackburn, where North End were beaten 3–0 on New Year's Day, and where West Bromwich Albion went down 4–1. The Arsenal, however, had their revenge in the return fixture, routing the champions late in the season by 5–1. The news staggered the Rovers' supporters, who could scarcely believe the published reports, but the explanation of the debacle was that the Gunners on that Monday afternoon were in such irresistible mood that they seldom allowed their opponents to settle on the ball. Grant, the old Southport Central amateur, scored three of the goals, and the other two were credited to Flanagan, who for once led Crompton a merry dance. The success over West Bromwich atoned for an earlier failure at the Hawthorns. North End managed to divide the points at Deepdale. Sunderland, generally a difficult side to conquer, won 3–0 at Roker Park, as did Manchester City at Hyde Road, but while Sunderland shared the spoils at Blackburn, Manchester City were beaten at Ewood by 2–0. Aston Villa had to surrender four points that season to the Rovers, who romped home by 3–0 at Birmingham, a particularly gratifying

LEAGUE CHAMPIONS, 1911-12, 1913-14.

STANDING: A. WALMSLEY, G. CHAPMAN, J. SIMPSON, P. J. SMITH, R. CROMPTON, W. AITKENHEAD, R. HOLMES (TRAINER), J. W. DAWSON (DIRECTOR).

SITTING: W. ANTHONY, J. ORR, A. ROBINSON, A. COWELL, W. BRADSHAW, W. CAMERON.

performance. Bury, Liverpool, Oldham and Everton were other victims of the double event. On all hands it was admitted that the Rovers were worthy of the high honour to which they had so often aspired and had at last attained.

One would imagine that there would be little wrong with a side capable of winning the blue riband of the League, but the directors, wise in their day and generation, were not unmindful of the circumstance that Simpson was without an ideal partner and that the outside left position required strengthening, also they were faced with the problem of finding a reliable pivot. They dealt with their difficulties in a manner that clearly showed they were determined to get the best talent available. In January, 1913, it was announced that "Danny" Shea, of West Ham, and "Joe" Hodkinson, of Glossop, had been signed, these two players costing the club about £3,000 in transfer fees, of which £2,000 was in respect of the London star.

Simpson and Shea were not long in assimilating, and the Rovers were now in the happy position of possessing a "golden wing" second to none for brilliancy and skill. On the other flank a sympathetic understanding developed between Latheron and Hodkinson, which added to the potency of the attack, but the connecting link at centre-forward still lacked perfection. W. Cameron, Aitkenhead, Orr, McGhie and Chapman each filled the position. Of the five, Chapman was the most effective; he also rendered acceptable service as an emergency full-back and at centre-half. Naturally, it was a disappointment that the Rovers were dethroned from the leadership. They finished fifth this season (1912-13), with 45 points. Until the second week in December they were at the head of the table. Then they sustained five consecutive defeats. It was anything but a merry Christmas for the "Blue and Whites," whose misfortunes were attributable not to loss of skill, but to an appalling injured list, relating to no fewer than 10 players, including Crompton, Cowell, Smith, Bradshaw, Davies and Orr. The New Year, though, saw a marked improvement, coinciding with the acquisition of Shea and

Hodkinson and the recovery of the injured men. Indeed, from the beginning of January to the end of the campaign only one League reverse was chronicled, and the team illuminated their path with a number of brilliant feats, standing third in the list of goal-getters in the division during a winter of rather heavier scoring than usual. In some cases the Rovers literally ran away with their opponents. For example, in the early stages Tottenham Hotspur were defeated 6–1, Bolton Wanderers 6–0, Bradford City 5–0, and, after the New Year, Middlesbrough 5–2, Liverpool 5–1, Oldham 7–1, and Chelsea 6–1. On the other hand, but two sides scored four goals in a game against the "Blue and Whites," Liverpool winning 4–1 at Anfield, and West Bromwich 4–2 at Ewood. In a friendly match on their opponents' ground the Rovers gave Westmorland County a sample of their prowess by winning 11–0.

Aitkenhead, Latheron, Shea, Simpson, and Chapman, all names that recall delightful recollections, were the principal marksmen. "Billy" Bradshaw enhanced his reputation, and in five penalties mystified opposing goal- keepers. Percy Smith was again a fine spoiler and feeder, and Albert Walmsley was as regularly useful and able as any half-back in the kingdom. As usual, Robinson, Crompton and Cowell proved themselves a redoubtable trio.

The flourish with which they opened their campaign in the autumn of 1913 furnished convincing evidence that the Rovers' deposition from their lofty pinnacle in the previous season was due more to accident than to any real inability of the side as a whole, and at the end of the following April they had won the coveted championship for the second time in three years. That wonderful pre-war achievement is one of the brightest episodes in the history of the club. When the "Blue and Whites" garnered 11 out of a possible 12 points in the first month and 17 out of 20 by the end of October, justification was given for the huge amounts spent on transfer fees. The bold policy of the directors in building up a winning side was warmly applauded. November, though, was responsible for a temporary set-back, three of the five games being lost, all on tour, while on the third Saturday

Photo by Burton & Garland, Ltd., Blackburn

E. G. LATHERON.

Photo by Burton & Garland, Ltd., Blackburn

J. HODKINSON.

F. DUCKWORTH.

Photo by Burton & Garland, Ltd., Blackburn

T. SUTTIE.

in December Manchester United secured a narrow victory at Ewood Park. A quick recovery atoned for that lapse. Only for one brief week was the Rovers' predominance in jeopardy. Then they went unfalteringly forward to the goal of their desire. During the game with Sheffield United at Bramall Lane, where they dropped their first point of the season, three of the Blackburn players were injured, and a spectator died through the heat. As Chapman, troubled with muscular rheumatism, was not as penetrative as usual, Aitkenhead replaced him as leader of the attack, and opened splendidly by performing the "hat trick" against North End.

Subsequently there were developments in regard to the playing staff. Early in the New Year, Clennel was the subject of a sensational transfer to Everton for £1,500. A few weeks later came the equally startling news that the Rovers had signed Percy Dawson, the famous centre-forward of the Heart of Midlothian. This coup, which took the football world by surprise, was another illustration that the East Lancashire club were determined to get the best men available to remedy defects in the team. Dawson, a native of the Newcastle district, had been three years with the Hearts, and was described as the best centre-forward in Scotland. He took some time to settle down amid the strange atmosphere which surrounds English football. While wearing the blue and white colours he was responsible for many grand displays, though his effectiveness was often impaired by the remarkably close shadowing he received from opponents, some of whom were none too scrupulous in the methods they employed to knock him off his game. The rare pace at which he covered the ground was very deceptive, and many of his shooting feats were not only spectacular but magnificent. On his day and at his best, Dawson was superb. No official information was forthcoming as to the transfer fee, but there is reason to believe that at the lowest it was £2,000 and at the highest not far short of £3,000.

Thus the Rovers' attack had cost the club £7,000, reckoning the sums paid for Simpson, Hodkinson and Shea, and the infinitesimal £25 that Grangetown received for Latheron eight years previously. As a matter of fact, "Eddie" was almost worth his weight in gold. In this memorable season (1913-14) he had no superior in footwork, and in the opinion of competent judges was the best inside-left in England.

With 51 points (their record number) the Rovers were no fewer than seven ahead of their old rivals, Aston Villa, who were second. Middlesbrough, West Bromwich Albion and Oldham Athletic each had 43 points, the North Riding club being allotted third place on goal average. The Rovers registered 78 goals, a feat unequalled by any other team in the division that winter; while the 42 obtained by opponents was one more than the previous lowest recorded against the "Blue and Whites," in the second season of the League, and the second lowest of any club in the division in 1913-14. Bradford City surrendered only 40 goals, but had an equal number scored against them. The Villa's goals were 65 against 50, and Middlesbrough's 77 against 60. Of the 38 games the Rovers won 20 and lost 7, sharing the points on the other 11 occasions.

The previous winter the "Blue and Whites" had done pretty much as they liked with seven opposing elevens, but this time there were greater obstacles to overcome. Most of the teams they conquered died gamely. Four, though, were nearly annihilated. North End after losing 5–0 at Ewood Park at Christmas were vanquished 5–1 at Deepdale on Boxing Day, and the other three outstanding results made a Roman holiday for the Blackburn spectators, who saw Liverpool beaten 6–2, and Middlesbrough and Everton each trounced 6–0. Shea (28 goals) and Latheron (13) were the men who did most mischief as marksmen, with Chapman and Aitkenhead next in order of merit.

A. Robinson, who was a sure shield behind Crompton and Cowell, had distinguished himself with Gainsborough Trinity in the Second Division of the League before he became a Rover in 1911. A native of Hulme, Manchester, at 17 he was under the bar for Chapel-en-le-Frith. In December, 1908, he went to Gainsborough, a year later was given his place in the first eleven, and from that time to severing his connection with the club to come to Ewood he never missed a match.

Walmsley, Smith and Bradshaw, as an intermediate trio, rendered magnificent service. While their styles were dissimilar, they were a remarkably effective file. Albert Walmsley, a native of Blackburn, after playing with local junior clubs, gained further experience with Darwen for two seasons prior to joining the "Blue and Whites" in 1907. A rare worker, with consistency as an outstanding characteristic, he was keenness personified. As he made little fuss on the field, he did not always catch the eye, but close students of the game appraised him at his true value. Strong and bustling, Percy Smith was ever in the thick of the fray. At times he figured successfully as a forward, but it is as a centre-half that he will be chiefly remembered. When he came to Blackburn in 1910 he had been associated with North End for seven years. Full of energy and possessing a head that was a magnet for the ball, he retained his position by sheer merit. Preston must often have realised that they made a great mistake in parting with such a talented exponent. On the left flank, "Billy" Bradshaw, born at Padiham, and the most prominent member of a well-known football family, was renowned for his artistic footwork and subtle support of the forwards. Obtained from Accrington Stanley, he first appeared for the Rovers in a friendly game against Bradford City on the occasion of the opening of the Valley Parade enclosure, and made his League debut at Wolverhampton in mid-September, 1903. For four years he operated at left-half, and from October, 1907, to the end of the season was a capable emergency outside-left. But he preferred his original position, to which he returned in 1908. When a penalty for the Rovers was signalled, opposing custodians had reason to dread Bradshaw's marksmanship, for in his first 20 shots from the spot he only missed scoring twice. Among his trophies are four international caps.

As forward, half-back and full-back, George Chapman was a host in himself. Fast and eager, he revelled in his work, and could live through the hardest game. None who witnessed it will ever forget his thrilling dribble in the stirring cup-tie with Manchester United in March, 1912, probably the most exciting match even seen at Ewood Park. With defeat staring them in the face, the Rovers by a superhuman effort by Simpson and Aitkenhead equalised in the closing minutes. During the extra time Chapman roused the mammoth crowd to a frenzy by dribbling half the length of the field, colliding with and beating both backs, and then crashing into the goalkeeper, who had rushed out to intercept him. Both went to earth. As he fell the gallant Blackburn centre-forward, with a last effort, shot out his foot, hitting the ball, which rolled slowly towards the untenanted goal. At the time, the custodian, one of the backs and Chapman were in a heap on the ground, with no other player near the scene. When after a few seconds—which seemed hours—the ball trickled over the goal-line between the posts, a policeman standing behind the net whipped off his helmet and waved it wildly. On receiving that signal the crowd went into ecstasies; so deafening and prolonged was the cheering that it was heard miles away from Ewood. Chapman's glorious effort gave the Rovers the lead, and he had the joy of adding another goal, which enabled his side to triumph by 4–2. On September 30th, 1916, when Rochdale paid their first League visit to Blackburn, the same player created a record for the club and ground by scoring six goals in succession (three in each half), the "Blue and Whites" winning 6–1.

The unleashing of the dogs of war in August, 1914, was the preliminary to the mightiest armed conflict the world has seen and, let us hope, ever will see. It was expected that football would close down, as there was a sterner game to be undertaken; but in the national interest it was deemed expedient for the sport to continue. On reflection it appears to have been a wise decision, though at the time it was adversely criticised. From a Blackburn standpoint the season was disappointing. The Rovers fell from their high estate. Their resolution was unshaken, but casualties upset the side, and at the end of a gruelling eight months they were third on the list, with 43 points. This was the sixth time in seven

Some Past and Present Directors.

Back Row: R. Crompton, J. Forbes, T. A. Leaver, C. Cotton, R. B. Middleton (Secretary).
Front Row: E. Wood, H. Garstang, T. Gillibrand, L. Cotton, J. W. Dawson, J. H. Forrest, J. W. Walsh.

successive years that their pointage had exceeded 40, whereas only once prior to 1908-9 had they collected 40 points. Everton carried off the championship with 46 points, and Oldham Athletic were second with 45, so that there was precious little to choose between the first three.

Accidents to Dawson and Shea upset the poise of the forwards. In this crisis, Aitkenhead showed his adaptability by moving from half-back to make an excellent partner for Simpson, and in eight appearances at inside-right he scored nine goals, bringing his total to 73 since his League debut in 1906-7. Dawson was responsible for no fewer than 20 goals, with Latheron close on his heels with 17, which increased "Eddie's" total to 94. Shea found the net on 13 occasions. Simpson's football was remarkably clever and consistent, though his shooting was not as destructive as of yore. On the other wing, Hodkinson was also an accomplished performer. The war, of course, overshadowed everything, and with the ringing-down of the curtain the League competitions were discontinued until after the Armistice.

CHAPTER XIV. — ILLUSTRIOUS PLAYERS AND ADMINISTRATORS.

Messrs. L. and C. Cotton — Lavish Expenditure on Ground and Team — Snobbishness at an International — Giants of the Game: Messrs. J. Forrest, J. Forbes and R. Crompton — The Present Board of Directors — Mr. Middleton's Fine Service to Blackpool and the Rovers.

T HE exalted position attained by the Rovers' F.C. in sporting circles is due not only to the players who have distinguished themselves on the field, but to the fine example set by the gentlemen who have guided its destinies. The high standard implanted by the amateurs who founded the club has been worthily maintained by their successors. At one time or another such men as Mr. John Lewis, Mr. Richard Birtwistle, Dr. Morley, Alderman Lawrence Cotton, Mr. Clement Cotton, Mr. J. H. Forrest, Mr. John Forbes, Mr. J. W. Walsh and Mr. Robert Crompton, to select a few names at random, have been concerned not merely with its deliberations but have increased its power and influence. Though he has not been officially connected with the Rovers for some years, Mr. Lewis, who founded the club, still takes a fatherly interest in its affairs. As a player he had not the privilege of figuring in a final, but as a referee he had charge of three finals, being the first "outsider" to control that important contest. Previously the referees had been chosen from the F.A. Council, of which Mr. Lewis was not then a member, but of which he is now a vice-president.

Dr. Morley and Mr. Richard Birtwistle as chairmen served the club with a fidelity akin to devotion. When the last-named retired in 1905 he was succeeded by Mr. Lawrence Cotton, who pursued such an active, vigorous and successful policy that he earned the title of "The maker of the modern Rovers." In the next ten years about £33,000 was spent on the equipment of Ewood Park, and between 1906 and 1914 £12,250 was expended in obtaining players. Mr. Cotton did not believe in half-measures. He visioned an A1 ground and a first-class team. With the willing co-operation of his fellow-directors he secured both. His bold policy was attended by gratifying results. It was typical of Mr. Cotton that after the railway company had refused to run excursions to Liverpool in 1912 for a semi-final in which the Rovers were participating, the club at his instigation purchased 5,000 railway tickets and offered them to the Rovers' supporters at reduced rates, a generous action that was much appreciated. Like a bolt from the blue came the news of his resignation in February, 1919, after being actively identified with the club for over 28 years as a member of the committee, director and chairman. Mr. Cotton, who was then the Mayor of Blackburn, felt impelled to take this step on account of the pressure of civic and other duties, which prevented him from devoting the necessary time and attention to the heavy work of football reconstruction resulting from the war.

"It took five years," he pointed out in an interview, "to get the Rovers into the position they occupied in 1914, and it is going to take another five years to build up again. I feel that that arduous task should fall on the shoulders of a younger man who has more time at his disposal than I have." To the satisfaction of all concerned he accepted the presidency of the club, to which he was elected at the next annual meeting, and his brother, Mr. Clement Cotton, was appointed to succeed him as chairman. From boyhood the latter had been an enthusiastic supporter of the "Blue and Whites," had been a director since 1909, was a big shareholder, and no member of the Board discharged his duties more regularly and efficiently than the new chairman, who, like his brother, was a keen business man and a generous donor to many deserving causes. In him the Rovers always had a staunch friend and one who did everything in his power to encourage them to perform great deeds. On medical advice Mr. Clement Cotton retired from the chairmanship in 1921. At the annual meeting in June, the club, in recognition of his valuable services, paid him the highest honour they could confer by appointing him president in succession to his brother, who had passed away the previous month. Mr. Clement Cotton left the directorate because as chairman he became too excited at the matches, which had a prejudicial effect on his health. It is a melancholy coincidence that when the Rovers were defeated by the Corinthians in the first round of the Association Cup at the Crystal Palace, in January, 1924, the president, who was watching a Reserve game at Ewood Park, was so upset by the news that he had a seizure and died two days later.

His mantle as chairman descended to Mr. J. W. Walsh, a keen sportsman, who has been a member of the Board since March, 1911. He discharges his important duties conscientiously and zealously. Mr. Walsh possesses high qualifications for the position, and his gifts and experience are freely placed at the disposal of the Rovers' Club. With business acumen and administrative ability he combines tact and discretion. Under his shrewd and capable direction not only has the club continued to prosper, but its future is assured.

The Rovers still have the benefit of the wide experience and sage counsel of three of the most illustrious players who ever stepped on to a football field. Mr. J. H. Forrest, Mr. John Forbes and Mr. Robert Crompton constitute a famous trio. Their mighty deeds will never be forgotten. For a dozen years Mr. Forrest was a brilliant left half-back and a dependable full-back. He helped the Rovers to win the Association Cup five times. On each occasion he was singled out by the critics for special praise. In his first final against Queen's Park, Glasgow, in 1884, he scored the second goal, which decided the issue; the following year against the same side he opened the Rovers' account with a glorious shot. At 19,

Mr. Forrest gained the first of his 11 international caps, making his debut against Wales, at Wrexham. He was the first professional to assist England against Scotland, at Glasgow, in 1886. The Scottish Association, sticklers for amateurism, grimly protested against his inclusion. However, he duly turned out with the 10 amateurs, and was the victim of snobbishness that would not be tolerated nowadays. Mr. N. L. Jackson, who was in charge of the England side, insisted that the Rover should wear a tight-fitting white jersey in contrast to the loose white shirts of his colleagues. It is refreshing to add that P. M. Walter, the famous Old Carthusian, strongly disapproved of this distinction being drawn. In those far-off days Mr. Forrest received £1 per week from the Blackburn club, and as the F.A. paid him £1 for playing against the Scots the Rovers stopped his wages that week! One of the neatest and surest of footballers, he used his brains and rarely wasted a ball. His son, whose initials are also "J. H.," is a well-known playing member of the "Blue and Whites."

Mr. Forbes, who while with Vale of Leven appeared in five internationals for Scotland, made his debut with the Rovers in April, 1888, was captain of the side for four years, and in 1893 astonished the sporting world by retiring from active participation in the game. He was then at the zenith of his athletic prowess, and a left-back of unequalled resource. As an exponent of pure football he was without a rival. His volleying was perfect and his powers of recovery astonishing. Possessing all the qualities of a captain, Mr. Forbes' generalship, no less than his superb football, was invaluable to the side. With Vale of Leven he reached three final ties for the Scottish Cup, and he had the honour of twice leading the Rovers to victory in the final of the Association Cup competition—in 1890, when Sheffield Wednesday were vanquished 6–1, and in 1891 when Notts County were defeated 3–1 after a thrilling struggle. In each of these contests Mr. Forbes enhanced his reputation, especially against the powerful Notts forwards. As a player he had the distinction of being given a seat on the Rovers' committee, and for no fewer than 35 years has assisted in the government of the club, of which he is one of the most popular directors.

Few men in football have conferred so much lustre on their profession as Mr. Crompton. His unswerving loyalty to the Rovers throughout the whole of his playing career of 24 years (from October 10th, 1896, to the end of the season in 1920) and his brilliance in representative games form one of the brightest chapters of football history. During many bleak seasons when with an indifferent team the "Blue and Whites" had to struggle hard to retain their position among the seniors, this peerless defender and valiant captain was the inspiration and saviour of the side. His reward came later when the Rovers carried off the League championship twice in three years. As an international, Mr. Crompton holds the English record, with 34 caps; he was the first professional to captain an England eleven containing amateurs, and as captain of the England team he had the honour of being introduced to King George V. (then Prince of Wales), at the Crystal Palace in 1909, when he played the game of his life against Scotland. He began his dazzling international career at Ibrox Park, Glasgow, in 1902, on that tragic afternoon when the collapse of a stand caused the death of 25 spectators and injury to hundreds of others; in 1911 he was presented with his portrait by the Football Association in commemoration of his 25th international appearance. Mr. Crompton appeared in many Inter-League and other representative matches. Whether winning or losing he was always the same great-hearted player, was noted for his chivalry to his opponents, and remains, what he has ever been, a fine sportsman and a typical Englishman. In 1921 the Rovers' shareholders paid him a graceful tribute by electing him on the directorate, a position he still occupies.

Another gentleman who has rendered fine service to the club is Mr. Harry Garstang. After helping Blackburn Etrurians to win the Lancashire Amateur Cup, he joined the Rovers as a playing member, operating principally at centre-forward, For a season and a half he was a dashing leader of the attack, when health considerations caused his retirement from the field. Then, in 1904, he was elected on the Board of Directors, and for 21 years, with a break of 12 months, he served in that capacity until last June. During that long period Mr. Garstang did much hard work for the club, of which he is a zealous supporter.

The Board of Directors now consists of Mr. J. W. Walsh, chairman (elected in 1911 and appointed chairman on June 30th, 1921), Mr. J. Eddleston, J.P., vice-chairman (elected in 1917 and appointed vice-chairman in 1922), Mr. J. Forbes (elected in 1890), Mr. J. H. Forrest (elected in 1906), Mr. John Cotton (elected in 1920), Mr. W. H. Grimshaw (elected in 1920), Mr. R. Crompton (elected in 1921), Mr. J. H. Chadburn (elected in 1922), Mr. T. Birtwistle (elected in 1922), and Mr. W. Tempest (elected in 1925).

For over 22 years the club has possessed a very efficient secretary in Mr. R. B. Middleton. He succeeded Mr. J. Walmsley, whose predecessor was Mr. T. B. Mitchell. A native of Yorkshire, Mr. Middleton was originally a schoolmaster at Rotherham, played as an amateur for Wiston, whom he represented on the Sheffield Association, and was a capable referee. He left the scholastic profession to become secretary of Rotherham Town F.C., and at the end of two years accepted a similar position at Darwen. Next, out of 50 applicants, he was elected secretary of Blackpool F.C. It was an admirable choice, because by his foresight and ability he revolutionised the prospects and standing of the seaside club. There were many candidates for the secretaryship of the Rovers' F.C. when it became vacant in 1903. The applications were reduced to four, and at the meeting of the Board in July Mr. Middleton received the appointment.

While Blackpool were exceedingly sorry to lose him, they heartily congratulated him on his promotion and wished him every success in his new sphere. During the intervening period Mr. Middleton has thoroughly justified the confidence reposed in him. As a man and as an official he is held in the highest esteem. Genial without being effusive, he combines courtesy with shrewdness. With Mr. Middleton his word is his bond. He will have nothing to do with hedgers or shirkers. Straight as a die, he is pre-eminently a man whose influence counts. Since 1903 he has been a notable figure at Ewood Park, while his coups in securing famous players, in face of keen competition, have gained him much more than local renown. During his tenure of office the Rovers have twice been the League champions, narrowly missing that distinction on several other occasions; and Ewood Park has been transformed into one of the finest enclosures in the kingdom. The League Management Committee presented Mr. Middleton with a commemorative gold medal on his completion of 21 years as a football secretary, an honour that was richly deserved. In point of service with one club he is the doyen of Football League secretaries in Lancashire. He is a valued member of the Lancashire F.A., with which he has been connected for six years. Of the Rovers Mr. Middleton is intensely proud, and he rejoices that they are famed throughout the country for cleanness of play, high character, and the finest attributes of sportsmanship.

CHAPTER XV. — POST-WAR PERFORMANCES.

The War's Heavy Toll — Critical Situation — Management's Prompt Action — Side Strengthened in Every Department — Team Manager Appointed — A Token for the Future.

THE 1919-20 season found all the clubs remarshalling their forces to carry on where they had left off in the second year of the war. Some found the process fairly easy. Others, and none more so than the Rovers, discovered that the intervening years had levied their toll, and that there were gaps in the ranks that came near to being irreplaceable. Of the brilliant combination which had brought new honours to the old club just before the war, Eddie Latheron had died a soldier's death in France. In their report for 1918 the directors recorded his passing with deep regret, and added: "Coming to us as a boy in 1906 he gradually forced his way into the first team, and was generally regarded as the finest inside-left in the country. The familiar fair-haired figure, with its cheery smile, will be greatly missed when football is resumed." R. Crompton, perhaps the greatest figure in modern football, had arrived at the time of life when his rôle was that of the looker-on, though he still was ready to don the blue and white shirt; John Simpson, the nonpareil, would never put boot to ball again; and such stalwarts as Percy Smith, W. Bradshaw, Albert Walmsley, Alf. Robinson, George Chapman, W. Anthony, Johnny Orr, W. Aitkenhead, Alex. McGhie, Arthur Cowell, T. Suttie, and many another fine player had passed their prime, though several of them again turned out with the "Blue and Whites" when serious football was resumed.

In the annual report for 1920 the directors placed on record "the greatservices rendered to the club by Robert Crompton, W. Bradshaw, Albert Walmsley, Percy Smith and John Simpson, who will not be seen in the Rovers' colours next season. Robert Crompton, the greatest full-back of modern times, has been with the club nearly quarter of a century, and has rendered great service to the Rovers and the game of football generally. William Bradshaw has a 17-years' connection and Albert Walmsley 12, while Percy Smith's and John Simpson's is of shorter duration. All five have given of their best and, along with Eddie Latheron, formed the backbone of the team that won the League championship twice in three years. John Simpson's career has been brought to a close prematurely by illness. On April 27th a benefit was accorded him, from which he received over £1,100. In expressing their regret at the parting, the directors wish each of these players every success in the future."

W. Aitkenhead, a strong, clever footballer, did excellent service for the Rovers, whom he joined in 1907, after having had experience with Maryhill and Partick Thistle. For six or seven seasons he played regularly in the side, chiefly as an inside-forward, and besides scoring many goals by his clever marksmanship, was a skilful maker of openings. When the Rovers won the championship in 1912 for the first time in their history, Aitkenhead was chief goal-getter, a feat of distinction when the calibre of the men forming the Rovers' forward line in those days is considered. W. Anthony, outside-left, another member of the championship side, came to Ewood after playing with Nottingham Forest and Brighton and Hove, and was prominent for several seasons. Another winger who gave grand service was Alex. McGhie. He was signed in 1908-09 season and played occasionally after the war. A man of great versatility, he appeared at Ewood after experience with Liscard Central, Kirkdale and Ashton Town. While with Liscard he was the top scorer one season, though he only took part in half-a-dozen games. Quick to see and seize an opening, McGhie was a very useful forward who could play with success in most positions, though it

F.A. CUP SEMI-FINAL TEAM, 1925.

STANDING: J. CARR (SECY.-MANAGER), J. McKINNELL, D. ROLLO, R. SEWELL, T. WYLIE, M. ATHERTON (TRAINER).
SEATED: J. HULME, J. McINTYRE, H. HEALLESS (CAPTAIN), J. McKAY, A. CAMPBELL.
IN FRONT: J. CRISP, S. PUDDEFOOT.

was as an outside-right that he figured latterly. In the first Cup-tie after the war he scored the equalising goal against the Wolves at Ewood. "Johnny" Orr, a clever inside-forward with unusual skill in working the ball, joined the Rovers from an Edinburgh junior club. Like Anthony, he suffered from lack of inches, but he was a capital forward who knew the way to goal. He played many fine games in the years just before the war. Tommy Suttie was a full-back who seldom had an "off" day. Owing to the fact that he was reserve to such brilliant exponents as Crompton and Cowell, his League appearances were not as numerous as they otherwise would have been. Born at Lochgelly, he was a strong, dour defender, whose daring sometimes placed him in tight corners, but a fine man to have on a side. After the war, Suttie assisted Darwen and Great Harwood in the Lancashire Combination.

Thus, when the time came to make preparations for the resumption of football, it was seen that many an old stalwart would have to be replaced. While some were optimistic enough to believe that the club's resources were adequate, others doubted whether the eleven would be able to hold their own, particularly as the defence was identical with that which had done such fine service five or six years before—a long period in a footballer's career. In the attack were Danny Shea, Joe Hodkinson and Percy Dawson, so that here was the material on which to build a thrustful front line, but the outlook generally was problematical. When the season was opened with a four goals' win over such old rivals as North End, doubts and fears were allayed. But as the tournament progressed misgivings were borne out only too surely. Then the club's worries were increased by an unparalleled series of accidents to players. Early in December, David Rollo and Frank Reilly were obtained from Linfield and Falkirk respectively. This strengthening of resources brought an immediate improvement, the next two games being won. The rally, though, did not last, and after the "Blue and Whites" had been beaten by five goals to one by Notts County on Xmas Day, not a single match was won for ten weeks. To add to the humiliation, the Rovers were knocked out of the Cup competition in the first round by their old Cup rivals, Wolverhampton Wanderers, then an average Second Division side.

The management wisely decided on bold measures, and in spring, 1920, the football world was given a new topic of conversation by the courage shown by the Ewood directors in face of one of the most critical situations in the club's history. On February 14th, Ronald Sewell, of Burnley, made his debut with the side; and only nine days later Levy Thorpe, also from Turf Moor, and Norman Rodgers, of Stockport County, appeared for the first time. Strengthened in every department, the team gradually turned the corner until at last there was a glimmer of hope that descent into the lower division might be evaded. Every man played his part splendidly in the battle, but the one who caught the imagination was Rodgers, who scored with amazing regularity, and in the eleven matches in which he appeared before the end of that fateful season obtained thirteen goals. It was a desperate struggle to the very last moment. An unusually large number of clubs were concerned in the fight against relegation, and when the crowd at Ewood Park, anxiously awaiting news of other games after they had seen the Rovers thrash Sheffield United by four goals in the last match, heard how other lowly-placed sides had gathered points, there was gloomy foreboding. Then came the news that Notts County had lost on their own field to Manchester United, and word spread like wildfire that the Rovers were safe. So close was the struggle among the bottom clubs that year that had any one of the five next nearest to the two relegated won one match less, they would have descended into the lower section.

The experiences of this season (1919-1920), when £13,560 was spent in obtaining new players, showed clearly that the Rovers would have to build afresh with an eye to the future. While several tried servants were allowed to go, the nucleus of a side which it was hoped would restore the fortunes of the "Blue and Whites" was retained. Besides such men as Rollo, Reilly, Sewell, Rodgers and Thorpe, players like Fred Duckworth, "Dick" Walmsley, Ernest Hawksworth, Harry Healless, T. Heaton and P. B. Holland, who had proved their mettle during the year, were kept, and it was hoped that in these the club would find a team worthy of its traditions.

When autumn came round again, there was a general belief that the 1920-21 season would see the old club re-establish itself among the "big powers" of football. But once more the Rovers were faced by an almost insuperable problem in the matter of injuries. "Dick" Walmsley, a native of Blackburn, whose magnificent form at right-back had won more than local notice, so badly hurt his knee while in light training that he never kicked a ball all that season in a serious match. Thus the career of one of the most promising defenders of post-war football—he was a fine kick, amazingly fast, and a prodigious worker— was cut off just as it looked like coming to fruition. The club, therefore, had to face the season with an already swollen sick list. The side was decidedly a better combination than that which opened the previous campaign, but though the team played very convincingly at times, the club finished with a very moderate place in the table. In one sense, however, it was a successful period: that is, in the discovery of men to meet the need of the hour. Rodgers was badly hurt, while J. McDonald, a clever Glasgow man, who somehow never quite touched his best at Ewood Park, also had to undergo an operation for leg trouble. The crowning misfortune came almost in the last week of the season when Fred Duckworth, whose form since the war had been so brilliant that he had played in two Victory Internationals, broke his arm in two places, ironically enough in a charity match with Burnley. A smallish man who was much more powerful than he looked, Duckworth was the idol of the Blackburn crowd, who had watched his progress from a young amateur in a local league. Cool and self-reliant, he was another of the Rovers' discoveries. That two local men in Walmsley and Duckworth, partners in defence, should blossom into such fine footballers only to have their careers cut short so suddenly, was a big blow to the club.

Another well-known figure who passed off the Rovers' stage

CENTRAL LEAGUE TEAM, 1924-25.

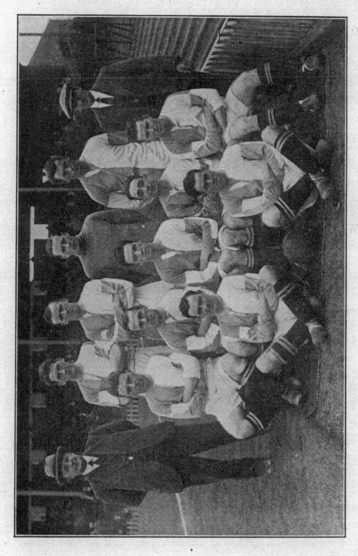

BACK ROW: J. ENTWISTLE, R. ROXBURGH, S. DIXON, J. CRAWFORD, P. HOPE, D. CROOK (TRAINER)
MIDDLE ROW: E. HAWKSWORTH, P. HOLLAND, E. HARPER, W. McCLEERY, F. MORTON.
FRONT ROW: D. LOW, A. POOL.

that year was Danny Shea, never after the war the tremendous match-winning force he was in the Simpson era. For all that, "Danny" will never be forgotten by Blackburn people who were electrified scores of times by his delicate dribbling and that sudden, wheeling shot of his which used to hurl the ball towards the goal like a thunderbolt. In place of these men there were discovered a number of promising young players, among whom the most conspicuous were Tom Wylie, now in his fifth year with the side, J. Donnelly, A. Pool and W. Simpson—two wing half-backs from Annan—Tommy Heaton, Billy Watson, B. Ralphs, J. McKinnell, and J. McCall. Wylie, a plucky little Scot from Darvil, has been a rare post-war "find." Though some local people do not appear to appreciate it, he is one of the steadiest left-backs in present-day football. Heaton, another local, played some grand games at left-half, before being transferred to Oldham Athletic, for whom he appeared against the Rovers in a Cup-tie last season. Watson, a Darwen half-back, was a clever footballer, afterwards transferred to Accrington Stanley. Ralphs, a winger from the Midlands, hardly lived up to his promise. McKinnell and McCall came as a complete left wing from Dumfries. All these won more or less permanent place in the side. About this time E. Hawksworth, who was secured for a comparatively small fee from Rochdale, reached his best as an accomplished and dangerous inside-left. Quick and clever on the ball, he was a very difficult man to stop, and the injury which blighted his playing career probably robbed him of an international cap.

It was felt that the 1921-22 season, with a reinforced playing staff, could be faced with more equanimity than had either of the other two post-war years. But again experience was to show that the club's fortunes were still in a state of flux. The season was indifferently successful from a playing standpoint, the side finishing eighth from the bottom. The directors were confronted chiefly with problems regarding the attack, in itself an illuminating commentary on the manner in which the war had changed the Rovers' outlook. In these circumstances the management wisely came to the conclusion that more new blood was necessary. Accordingly two new inside-forwards were obtained, John McIntyre, from The Wednesday, and John McKay, from Glasgow Celtic, who was accompanied to Ewood by Archie Longmuir, a hard-working centre-forward with a tremendous drive in his boots, who rendered useful service on the right wing before leaving for Wrexham. These men wrought an immediate improvement. The club, though, was still under a cloud, for McKay, who proved himself from his first game one of the cleverest men who ever wore the blue and white livery, was so badly injured that in all he missed over 20 matches, while Rodgers, never the same player after his first operation for knee trouble, had again to receive treatment for that injury. Towards the end of this season there was something of a "nine days' wonder" in Rovers' football in the way Ronald Howarth, of Lower Darwen, after appearing in a local junior league, adapted himself to First Division requirements by leading the attack with much success towards the end of the campaign. He hardly maintained his form, and left Ewood Park for Hull City. This year was notable in that the Rovers followed the example of other big clubs by engaging a team manager to look after the well-being and accommodation of the players. Mr. John Carr, the old Newcastle United international full-back, was appointed, and there is no doubt that his influence has done a great deal of good.

Hope springs eternal, and the coming of the 1922-23 campaign was welcomed all the more warmly because it was felt that at last the "Blue and Whites" were once again on the highway to success. During the close season Dicky Bond, the famous right-winger, who earned laurels with North End and Bradford City, had thrown in his lot with the Rovers. It was the general hope that with one weak spot strengthened the attack would be better armed for its task of getting goals. The defence had been improved, too, by the acquisition of Edwin Davis, of Huddersfield Town. These high hopes were only to be half realised, however. At times the eleven showed their mettle by winning by big margins—five goals were scored against Everton and Albion—but there were too many off-days, and within ten weeks of Christmas four opposing teams each scored five goals, so that on the whole the season had few distinctive aspects. Still, there were two noteworthy features. The first was McIntyre's achievement of scoring four goals in five minutes against Everton at Ewood Park on September 16th, 1922, which feat has been claimed as a record. In this game the "Blue and Whites" gave a magnificent exhibition. They were constantly in their opponents' territory in the first half, but the Everton charge had a charmed life, and the visitors were the first to score through Harrison, who converted a penalty kick awarded for hands. Just on the interval Healless equalised, The sensation came in the early part of the second period, which had been in progress 10 minutes when McIntyre with a fast rising drive gave the Rovers the lead. In the next two minutes he twice netted and at the end of 15 minutes again beat Fern, the Everton custodian, the four goals—all shot— being thus registered in five minutes. It was a brilliant performance, and enabled the home side to win by the substantial score of 5–1. The other was a fine victory over Aston Villa at Birmingham in the first round of the Cup competition. The goal was scored by Bond from a penalty, and great was the jubilation in the town when the news came through. Three weeks later, however, the Rovers, after running their opponents to a standstill, lost by the only goal to South Shields, in a second round replayed tie at Blackburn.

This year saw Frank Reilly, the centre half-back, numbered among those who sought pastures new. Though he was not so serviceable in his later years with the Ewood club, there can be no denying that he was an extremely capable half-back. Coming to Blackburn from Falkirk as a big-price transfer, Reilly, at his best, was a great centre-half, a stubborn defender and a clever initiator of attacks. With Thorpe and Heaton, who fell out of the limelight about the same time, he formed a most useful middle line. Thorpe, who captained the side for some time, was a "canny" right half-back who knew football inside out, and he was as good in attack as in defence. Heaton's place at left-half was taken by McKinnell, who suddenly found his true position when played in the intermediate line. Reilly was succeeded by Stanley Dixon, who was secured in March, 1923, from Newcastle, as an inside forward, and later won encomiums by the way he stood in the breach at half-back. On the day Dixon made his debut, his partner was Crisp, who had been transferred from West Bromwich Albion the same week. Behind this wing, at right halfback, was A. Campbell, a recruit from Leadgate Park. He was also making his first appearance, and his steady progress warranted his inclusion as a regular member of the eleven.

A fine servant of the Rovers severed his connection with the club that year in Joe Hodkinson, who returned to the Lancashire Combination to finish his long, honourable career with Lancaster, the town of his birth. "Joe," as he was known to the Ewood crowd, came to Blackburn from Glossop in 1913. He cost about £1,000, a huge fee in those days, but he was worth every penny. Possessed of resource and exceptional pace, he rapidly earned a reputation which won him representative honours on several occasions. At times he appeared on the right flank, but it was as an outside-left that Hodkinson will be remembered. Like every other man, he had his off-days, but no club ever had a better servant than this fast, tricky Lancashire footballer.

Previous disappointment had made people rather chary of hoping for too much when the 1923-24 season came round. For one thing, it was urged that, as Dawson had departed, the club had no real centre-forward on its books. The emergency brought forth the man in Edward Harper, whom the Rovers discovered playing with Sheppey United, a junior organisation near London. He not only figured in every match, but set up a new post-war record for the club by scoring 18 goals. Big, strong, and a good shot, this youth was a real "find." The first half of the season saw the "Blue and Whites" perform in a way that suggested that at long last the end of the tournament would find the club in a position in the chart commensurate with tradition. But there was a decline, and in addition the Rovers unwillingly provided the sporting world with a new sensation by being beaten by Corinthians, the well-known amateur combination, in the first round of the Cup competition. It is one of the tragedies of the footballer's life that the man who has been the popular idol often passes out of the public eye almost unnoticed. This was the case with Norman Rodgers, who severed his playing connection with the Rovers in 1924. It was largely Rodgers' brilliance that saved them in the disastrous 1919-20 season, and though recurring knee troubles shortened his career, he will not soon be forgotten by Blackburn people. A superb shot, he was a delightful footballer, who got his results without fuss, and he never did the spectacular when plain, honest method would serve. Rodgers was one of the biggest figures in the club's post-war history, and he will take an honoured place in the long list of famous Rovers,

Last season the "Blue and Whites" had a chequered career, but redeemed themselves to some extent by their progress in the Association Cup competition, in which, as stated in Chapter X., they established a national record by appearing in a semi-final for the 12th time. With 35 points (10 fewer than the previous season) they finished 16th in the League, or seventh from the bottom. Of the 42 games 11 were won, 18 lost and 13 drawn, 53 goals being scored as compared with 66 obtained by opponents. For the greater part of the tournament the attack were without a real leader. This had an unsettling effect, especially as five of the seven men experimented with in the middle were moved from their accustomed places in the hope that the position would be adequately filled. The connecting link, however, remained unstable until S. C. Puddefoot, of Falkirk and formerly of West Ham, was signed in February last. His individual brilliance and clever leadership produced immediate results. In the next half-dozen League games but one reverse was chronicled, as against two wins and three draws. Unfortunately, there was then a relapse, with defeat in five of the last nine matches.

McIntyre and McKay, with a dozen apiece, claimed 24 of the 53 goals registered by the Rovers in the League campaign. Puddefoot and McCleery had five each, Crisp and Hulme four each, Harper and Holland three each, Healless two, and Roscamp and Brayshaw one each, Jones putting through his own goal in the match with Birmingham. In the Association Cup-ties goals were scored by McKay (3), Puddefoot (2), Hulme (2), and Campbell and Crisp, one each. McIntyre had a great week-end in the early part of the season, when he registered five goals in three days against Burnley and Liverpool. Hulme, a promising recruit from York City, developed into a dashing outside-right. He had the distinction of being the sole member of the side to appear in the whole of the League matches. Sewell missed but one and Wylie two. Rollo increased his total of international caps to 14, while Wylie had made 102 successive appearances in League and F.A. Cup contests prior to April 22nd, when he was absent from the Rovers' eleven, who suffered their heaviest reverse of the season at Burnden Park, where Bolton Wanderers triumphed 6–0. The Blackburn team's biggest win, 7–1 over Birmingham at Ewood Park, was recorded at the beginning of the same month, the visitors being handicapped by injuries. In R. Roxburgh, of Newcastle United, and P. Hope, of Norwich City, the club appear to have found excellent reserve backs.

H. Healless, the captain and the only Blackburn man in the side, played magnificently at centre-half, where his speed, strength and skill were of the utmost value in many a stern encounter. He thoroughly earned the recognition he received from the authorities. Further honours will probably come his way. At wing-half Roscamp, McKinnell, Campbell, and D. Low (of New Harrington Swifts) rendered more than useful service. At inside-right, centre-forward or outside-left Crisp gave of his best, while W. McCleery, from Belfast, was a distinct success as an inside-forward. W. Brayshaw, from Denaby United, on making his debut with the "Blue and Whites" against Sunderland at Ewood Park on April 18th, created an excellent impression at inside-right, and had the satisfaction of opening the scoring at the end of 37 minutes, Buchan equalising with a header in the second half. On April 22nd the club signed A. Rigby, of Bradford City, one of the finest outside-lefts in the Second Division. Young, clever and fast, Rigby went to Bradford from Crewe Alexandra. He is expected to prove a valuable acquisition. J. Crawford, a custodian from Alloa, is another new man of more than average merit.

As the directors are pursuing a steadily progressive policy, it is anticipated that the golden jubilee season will witness a further revival in the fortunes of the Rovers. Those in authority are alive to the importance of fielding an eleven worthy of maintaining the great traditions of the club. With that end in view weak places in the side have been strengthened. In the ranks there are tried men whose football skill is unquestioned, also a number of young players of undoubted promise. From this blending of experience and youth the happiest results are confidently expected. That that confidence will be more than justified by the side's performances is the sincere wish of all interested in the welfare of a club that for fifty years has kept not only its flag flying, but has borne an honoured name at home and abroad.

ASSOCIATION CUP FINALS.

March 25th, 1882 :
Old Etonians, 1; Blackburn Rovers, 0.
(At Kennington Oval).

March 29th, 1884 :
Blackburn Rovers, 2; Queen's Park, Glasgow, 1.
(At the Oval).

April 4th, 1885 :
Blackburn Rovers, 2; Queen's Park, Glasgow, 0.
(At the Oval).

April 3rd, 1886 :
Blackburn Rovers, 0; West Bromwich Albion, 0.
(At the Oval).

April 10th, 1886 — Replay :
Blackburn Rovers, 2; West Bromwich Albion, 0.
(At Derby).

March 29th, 1890 :
Blackburn Rovers, 6; Sheffield Wednesday, 1.
(At the Oval).

March 21st, 1891 :
Blackburn Rovers, 3; Notts County, 1.
(At the Oval).

A NATIONAL RECORD.

The Rovers have reached the Semi-Final stage of the Association Cup Competition 12 times, a national record.

LEAGUE CHAMPIONS.

The Rovers won the League Championship in the seasons 1911-12 and 1913-14.

LANCASHIRE SENIOR CUP SUCCESSES.

They have won the Lancashire Senior Cup on 11 occasions.

In Memoriam : R. B. Middleton

The death of Mr. R. B. Middleton, which occurred after this volume was in the press, occasioned deep regret. Following a long illness, he passed away at his residence in Mavis Road on September lst. Mr. Middleton, who was 57 years of age, had been secretary of the Blackburn Rovers Football Club since July, 1903, and was noted for the fidelity and zeal with which he discharged his duties.

The Board of Directors, at a meeting on September 3rd, expressed their profound sympathy with the bereaved family and placed on record their high appreciation of the services rendered by Mr. Middleton to the club. The representative gathering at the funeral and the beautiful display of flowers testified to the esteem in which the late secretary was held by his colleagues in the football world as well as by his personal friends. In Chapter XIV. allusion is made to Mr. Middleton's career as a football official.

The Directors at a meeting on September 30th, 1925, appointed Mr. J. Carr secretary-manager.